Miniature Golde

Miniature Golde
Complete Owne

Miniature Golden Retriever book for care, costs, feeding, grooming, health and training.

by

George Hoppendale

and

Asia Moore

Author: George Hoppendale
Author & Dog Whisperer: Asia Moore
www.K-9SuperHeroesDogWhispering.com
www.MustHavePublishing.com
www.KnowsToNose.com

Published by: PESA Publishing

Table of Contents

About the Authors

George Hoppendale is an experienced writer and a true animal lover. He enjoys writing animal books and advising others how to take care of their animals to give them a happy home.

Asia Moore is an animal lover, professional Dog Whisperer and experienced Author who has written more than 250 breed specific books.

Asia lives on Vancouver Island, off the west coast of British Columbia, in Canada, and believes that with the right training, all humans and dogs can live together in harmony.

She and her dog whispering detective team, which includes an 11-year-old Shih Tzu named Boris, teaches dog psychology and offers canine matchmaking services to humans around the world for those thinking about sharing their life with a dog, in order to help find the right match.

Asia also trains humans and rehabilitates canines who have developed behavioral issues by teaching dog psychology to human guardians, in order to prevent or help alleviate problem behaviors that arise through common as well as unusual misunderstandings between humans and their canine counterparts so that everyone can live a happy and stress-free life together.

Visit Asia online at the following locations:
www.K-9SuperHeroesDogWhispering.com
www.KnowsToNose.com
www.MustHavePublishing.com

Chapter 1: Introduction

It's important to gather as much information as possible before you take the plunge to share your home with a furry friend. While humans and dogs have been relying on one another for more than 30,000 years, it's very important that you choose the canine companion that is best suited to your particular lifestyle.

The Miniature Golden Retriever Dog Complete Owner's Manual will answer the questions you may have when researching this designer canine. If you are considering sharing your home with the friendly and highly intelligent Miniature Golden Retriever, this manual is for you.

Learn all about this designer dog, including facts and secrets, and how to care for every stage of the Miniature Golden Retriever's life.

This book contains all the information you need, from choosing a breeder and finding the perfect puppy to how to care for an aging dog.

In addition, you will learn about transitioning through house breaking, adolescence, daily care, health problems inherent in the breed, feeding, grooming, training, first commands and beginner hand signals as well as the end of their life, so that you can make an educated decision when deciding whether or not the energetic and loyal Miniature Golden Retriever is the breed for you and your family.

Please keep in mind, when reading this book, that it contains generalizations that hold true for most breeds, plus a great deal of highly valuable dog whispering techniques that have been honed and perfected from over 40 years experience while working with a wide variety of canine breeds and other animals in the wild.

If you want to have the best relationship with your canine family member, it is far more important that you realize the value inherent in all the many positive tips, tricks and dog whispering expertise this book contains, than it is to learn, for instance, what color a particular breed's coat may be.

While it can be fun and interesting to hear about the ancient history of a breed or about particular inherited traits, or what celebrity may have owned one, learning the dog whispering techniques that can help avoid future behavioral problems, and the costs associated with then figuring out how to alleviate them, is far more valuable information for anyone considering sharing their home with a canine companion.

All of the dog whispering knowledge shared with you within the covers of this book can easily be applied to any breed of canine, because no matter what size, shape, color, purebred or hybrid pedigree may be involved, in order for every dog to be a happy and well-balanced member of your family, it's vital that they receive the right information and energy from their humans so that they can get a started off on the right paw.

^..^ Asia

Chapter 2: The Miniature Golden Retriever

The friendly *"Miniature Golden Retriever"* is a highly intelligent and athletic, medium-sized, designer, purebred canine hybrid which, despite their name, is NOT (as many might believe) simply a smaller version of the well loved Golden Retriever.

Most likely the aim of creating the Miniature Golden was to develop a companion sized version of the ever popular, larger sized Golden Retriever and while there is no standard for the Mini Golden and they are not registered with any of the standard purebred kennel clubs, this smaller Golden is also becoming popular and there is enough breeding activity to gauge what would be considered average for this hybrid creation.

This is a mix of Golden Retriever, Poodle and sometimes Cocker Spaniel that originated within the United States and while all breeders of this designer dog may have different ideas about what is the ideal percentage of each breed, most of them retain the look of the Golden Retriever.

While the appearance and size of the Miniature Golden Retriever will largely depend upon the appearance and size of both parents, generally speaking, this will be a medium-sized dog that requires a high amount of daily exercise.

The Miniature Golden will usually be a patient, friendly, high-energy dog that will be trusting and gentle with both family members and strangers alike.

This is a mix of three active, water-loving dogs, which means that the Miniature Golden will be athletic, energetic, playful and most usually friendly and gentle to everyone, while never missing an opportunity to swim.

This versatile dog's high intelligence and extreme eagerness to please means that the Miniature Golden may be a top performer in many canine sporting arenas, such as the Agility or Obedience competition ring.

As well, this dog's natural retrieving skill will also make for a highly competitive Flyball, Obedience, Water Retrieving or Field Trial participant and their love of water may also mean that this breed will be a tough competitor to beat in the dock diving arena.

If the Miniature Golden has any faults at all, it could be that guardians need to be aware that this dog's keen eagerness to please and intense focus on the task at hand, coupled with their love of retrieving, means that they do not know when to stop, and they may continue with the task at hand until they literally collapse from exhaustion.

For example, if you continue to fly that Frisbee they will continue to retrieve it, even in very hot weather and could drop from heat exhaustion before they quit. Or if you continue to throw that stick, even into very cold water, this dog will likely continue to retrieve it, even though they may be suffering from hypothermia.

Ideally, this energetic dog needs wide-open spaces where they can run, play and fetch. The Miniature Golden will love to go running or jogging and hiking with their guardians and if there is a body of water nearby, you may have difficulty keeping them out of it.

1. History/Origin of the Miniature Golden Retriever

While exactly what breeds are used to create the Miniature Golden can vary slightly, the puppies will usually be the result of crossing the Golden Retriever with the Poodle, a Golden Retriever and a Goldendoodle (Golden Retriever mixed with a ½ Poodle, ½ Golden) or a Golden Retriever, Poodle and Cocker Spaniel cross.

The specialist, hybrid breeding required to create the Mini Golden Retriever likely began because it was believed that there would be a marketplace for a dog that is smaller in stature than the very popular Golden Retriever, while keeping intact all the desirable character traits and temperament of the Golden.

In order to retain the look of the Golden, from a breeding point of view, this would mean maintaining a close genetic match to the Golden Retriever of between 50% and 75%.

For the purposes of this book, I will outline the characteristics, temperaments and health concerns of all three of these breeds for a complete overview of what a Mini Golden Retriever might become as a grown dog.

The Golden Retriever: was originally developed in 19th century Scotland, and bred by British aristocrats as a dual-purpose dog (retriever and companion) where the breed standard is heavier and stockier than the usual variety of Golden Retriever found in North America.

The improvement in firearms during the 1800s was largely instrumental in the development of today's Golden Retriever because with the improved shooting capacity of guns that were more accurate over a longer distance, came a problem for retrieving downed waterfowl or other birds over a greater distance of more difficult terrain, which resulted in many downed birds being lost in the field.

When it became evident that the pointer breeds were ineffective at the type of retrieval work that was required, Scottish enthusiasts began creating a specialized dog with the original breeding program beginning with crossing the now extinct Tweed Water Spaniel with a yellow-coated retriever and a red Setter.

The careful Golden Retriever breeding program also included the Irish Setter, the St. John's Water Dog (of Newfoundland), the blonde colored Bloodhound, and two more black coated retrievers to create the ultimate active and powerful retriever that also had a gentle mouth.

The playful Golden Retriever is certainly going to be a bouncy, energetic, fun loving dog with great stamina that loves attention and lives to run, retrieve and engage in endless activity with their family.

The Golden Retriever is an alert, patient, responsive, and loyal dog that is an excellent family companion. Although they do not make very good guard dogs, because they are a non-aggressive and love the company of everyone, they will certainly let you know if danger or an unknown person is approaching.

The Poodle: many people don't realize that the Poodle has been well known for very much longer than 400 or 500 years and may be one of the oldest breeds of canines known to man.

For instance, the ancient ancestral Poodle with the *"Lion Trim"* haircut appeared on ancient Greek and Roman coins during the time of Emperor Augustus in approximately 30 A.D.

As well, the Poodle was revered in pictures that were carved on many monuments, tombs and Palace walls and there is historic evidence of the intelligent Poodle seen in medieval manuscripts of the 15th, 16th and 17th centuries.

As the Poodle became well known as a distinct breed, they were bred down in size to become more of a companion dog, which resulted in the creation of the Miniature and Toy sizes of the breed.

Poodles have been used for a variety of jobs in history as hunters and retrievers, circus dogs, court and companion dogs for the rich and powerful. The Miniature Poodle was often used as a truffle dog for sniffing out the truffle used in French gourmet cooking.

Despite the Poodle's origins as a hunting and retrieving breed, they became well known for their abilities as performing dogs, and were widely distributed due largely to traveling gypsies who favored the Poodle above all others as a performing circus dog.

As a working retriever, the Poodle was originally considered an *"off-square"* breed, because their body was longer than it was tall, which is similar to most of today's retrieving breeds.

However, as the highly intelligent Poodle was such a superior circus act performer, which made them ever more popular with the traveling gypsies, with careful breeding practices, their body shape began to change to increase their ability for faster agility which was not possible with the longer retriever body shape. As a result, the original, longer Poodle body became more square shaped to improve the dogs' spinning and hind leg

acrobatic capabilities.
Interestingly, the standard, more square shape of all sizes of the Poodle breed is a result of improving their abilities as performing circus dogs, rather than as a hunting or retrieving breed, which makes the intelligent Poodle a multi-talented purebred canine.

While the Poodle has a delightful, loving temperament often described as alert, active, faithful, highly intelligent, and easily trainable, this is not a breed particularly well suited for the elderly or for humans that lead busy lives with long work schedules that keep them away from home.

In order for the Poodle to be well balanced psychologically, they demand a lot of attention and will not be happy spending only a few minutes with their humans each day.

While some breeds of dogs of lower intelligence might be just fine without receiving daily interesting activities to keep them busy and mentally challenged, the Poodle, with their lively and playful temperament, typically wants and needs to occupy much more of their guardian's time and energy by engaging in physical activities that also challenge them mentally.

A conscientious Poodle guardian will need to constantly be thinking of ways to challenge their bright and inquisitive canine companion and make their daily life interesting.

The Cocker Spaniel: this purebred sporting canine is descended from the English Cocker Spaniel and dates back to the 14th century and the Cocker Spaniel (Cocker) is a name given to both the American and English Cocker Spaniel.

This spaniel is built for speed and endurance and was first bred as a hunting dog in the United Kingdom where they were named after their superior ability for hunting the Eurasian Woodcock, which is a medium-sized wading bird with a long probing beak.

When the breed was brought to the United States in the early part of the 20th century, several physical changes were bred into the America Cocker to help the breed excel at hunting the American Woodcock, which is a smaller shore bird.

While both are closely related and both are called Cockers, the appearance between the American and the English Cocker Spaniel is distinctly different, with their smaller size, a shorter muzzle and rounder eyes that sets them apart from their English cousins.

This is a sensitive dog that will usually have a distinctively "doggy" smell about them and if not trained properly may suffer from separation anxiety, which can lead to them becoming loud barkers.

The Cocker is eager and willing to be trained and must never be treated harshly as they may become very nervous and frightened which can cause them to act defensively and fight back.

The water-loving Cocker Spaniel is an athletic, energetic, and playful dog that enjoys activity of any sort and can excel in many canine sports such as Agility and Obedience, Flyball, Water Retrieving or Dock Diving.

The sensitive Cocker Spaniel is certainly going to be a happy, energetic, fun loving dog with great stamina that lives to run, hunt and play, however, you need to keep in mind that this dog, when not trained properly and learning their position as a follower at a young age, can get into the habit of reacting defensively or aggressively when they are asked to do something they might not want to do.

There has been a great deal of in-breeding with this dog, which has resulted in many of these otherwise happy and friendly dogs becoming neurotic or aggressive, which means that carefully choosing your breeder will be paramount.

2. Miniature Golden Retriever Secrets

Rather than just a size variation on the Golden Retriever breed standard, this dog is a hybrid mix of three different dogs.

As the Golden Retriever is one of the three DNA elements of this hybrid companion, and their temperament and look is very similar to the Golden Retriever, this is likely why they were named the *"Miniature Golden Retriever"*.

The Miniature Golden Retriever is also known as the *"Little Retriever"*, the *"Petite Golden Retriever"* and the *"Comfort Retriever"*.

The name *"Comfort Retriever*" is the name trademarked by Kathy Burgess at Comfort Retrievers (who may have created the first Miniature Golden), which name has become synonymous with the breed.

Now, before we get any further into this book, it's important that you please understand that much of the content written in this book can be applied to EVERY dog, because when it comes right down to it, a dog is a dog no matter what size, shape, color, price tag or fancy purebred or hybrid name we humans might ascribe to them.

Every dog has a uniquely wonderful set of gifts to share with their human counterparts, if only us humans would listen. They "tell" us when they are unhappy, when they are bored, when they are under-exercised, yet often we do not pay attention, or we just think they are being badly behaved.

Many humans today are deciding to have dogs instead of children and then attempting to manipulate their dogs into being small (or large) furry children. This is having a seriously detrimental effect upon the health and behavior of our canine companions.

In order to be the best guardians for our dogs, we humans must have a better understanding of what our dogs need from us, rather than what we need from them, so that they can live in safety and harmony within our human environment.

Sadly, many of us humans are not well equipped to give our dogs what they really need and that is why there are so many homeless, abandoned and frustrated dogs.

As a professional dog whisperer who is challenged with the task of finding amicable solutions for canine/human relationships that have gone bad, once humans understand what needs to be changed, almost every stressful canine/human relationship can be turned into a happy one.

The sad part is that many humans are simply not willing to do the work and devote the time necessary to ensuring that their dog's needs are met. Almost all canine problems are a direct result of ignorance or unwillingness on the part of the canine guardian to learn what the dog truly needs.

First and foremost, our dogs need to be respected for their unique canine qualities.

For millennia, dog has been considered *"Man's best friend",* and in today's society, when we want to do the best by our canine companions and create a harmonious relationship, we humans need to spend more time receiving the proper training so that we can learn how Man can be dog's best friend.

A Miniature Golden Retriever is a dog and therefore can be "Man's or Woman's best friend" providing that we do the above.

That's the biggest *"secret"* because if the human treats the dog well and understands what the dog needs, the dog will be happy and the owner will be happy. This is a universal truth that applies to any dog, whether a Miniature Golden Retriever or any other breed.

For example, it is not possible to write a book specifically about *"How to train a Miniature Golden Retriever"* or specifically about what *"The first few days with your Miniature Golden Retriever"* will entail, etc., as while basic training techniques apply to every dog, every dog and every human/dog relationship will be unique.

For this reason, when referring to daily feeding, care, house training, behavioral training, socializing, etc., although there may be specific reference points relevant to the Miniature Golden Retriever breed, these chapters are NOT written to apply to a specific breed, as much of this information can be applied equally successfully to any dog breed.

Chapter 3: Choosing a Breeder

1. Locating a Reputable Breeder

Although a good breeder cannot guarantee the lifelong health of any puppy, they should easily be able to provide a prospective Miniature Golden Retriever guardian with plenty of information about the health of the puppy's parents. In the case of this hybrid companion, reputable breeders will have undertaken much research and careful study in order to develop Miniature Golden Retriever offspring that are suitable for people wanting smaller dogs that are easier to care for and generally live longer, while retaining all the desirable qualities of the standard Golden Retriever. **NOTE**: some believe that breeders who also use Cocker Spaniels in their Miniature Golden Retriever breeding program can invite more risk of creating puppies with undesirable characteristics that are not normally seen in a Golden Retriever (please refer to the section on the Cocker Spaniel under History).

For instance, some breeders have indicated that Miniature Golden Retrievers containing Cocker Spaniel parentage can be more prone to nipping and biting. Should this be the case, of course, a dog with these tendencies would be less family friendly and less suitable to be around small children.

Beyond determining what sort of parentage is involved in a breeding program, prospective guardians should definitely ask the breeder what sort of health tests have been carried out on the parents of a puppy they may be considering purchasing.

For instance, a reputable breeder will have had their breeding dogs tested for hip, thyroid, eye or other problems inherent in the breed and prospective puppy purchasers should always inquire about possible congenital problems the parents or grandparents of the puppy might have, including any premature deaths.

2. Meet the Parents

Meeting the mother and father of your new Miniature Golden Retriever puppy can tell you a great deal about what the temperament and demeanor

of your puppy will likely be when they grow into adulthood.
The puppy's personality or temperament will be a combination of what they experience in the early days of their environment when they are in the breeder's care, the genes inherited from both parents and how their guardians train and socialize them.

Visiting the breeder several times, observing the parents, interacting with the puppies and asking plenty of questions will help you to get a true feeling for the sincerity of the breeder.

The early environment provided by the breeder and the parents of the puppies as well as the environment, socializing and training provided by the puppy's new guardian can have a formative impact on how well your puppy will ultimately behave as an adult dog.

3. Questions to Ask a Breeder

Get to know your breeder by asking them why they decided to breed the Miniature Golden Retriever and how long they have been breeding. Ask if the breeder will permit you to visit their facility and will they give you a tour.

Ask the breeder if they own both breeding parents, or if they do not, ask if they are familiar with or have worked closely with both parents of the puppy you may be considering.

Ask how often the breeder allows the females and males to breed and reproduce, ask if the breeder will allow you to see the other dogs in the kennel and take notice whether the kennel is clean, well maintained and animal friendly.

Will the breeder permit you to see other adult dogs, or other puppies that the breeder owns, socialize together?

Pay attention to whether the breeder limits the amount of time that you are permitted to handle the puppies. A reputable breeder will be concerned for the safety and health of all their puppies and will only permit serious buyers to handle the puppies.

Check to find out if the breeder is registered or recognized by your local, state or national breed organization.

a) Medical Questions: every reputable breeder will certainly ensure that their puppies have received vaccinations and de-worming specific to the age of the puppies.

Always ask the breeder what shots the puppy has received and when it was last de-wormed and ask for the name of the breeder's veterinarian. If you discover that the breeder has not carried out any of these procedures or they are unable to tell you when the last shots or de-worming was carried out, look elsewhere.

Also ask to see the breeder's veterinarian report on the health of the puppy you may be interested in purchasing, and if they cannot produce this report, look elsewhere.

b) Temperament Questions: you will want to choose a puppy with a friendly, easy going and congenial temperament and your breeder should be able to help you with your selection. A good breeder will have noticed personality and temperament traits very early on in their puppies and should be able to provide a prospective purchaser with valuable insight concerning each puppy's unique personality.

Also ask the breeder about the temperament and personalities of the puppy's parents and ask what they have done to socialize the puppies. Ask how old the puppies must be before they can be taken to their new homes.

If the breeder is willing to let their puppies go any earlier than 10 weeks of age, they are more interested in making a profit than in the health of their puppies.

Always be certain to ask if a puppy you are interested in has displayed any signs of aggression or fear, because if this is happening at such an early age, you may experience behavioral troubles when the puppy becomes older.

c) Guarantee Questions: a reputable breeder will be interested in the lifelong health and wellbeing of all of their puppies and good breeders will want you to call them should a problem arise at any time during the life of your puppy. In addition, a good breeder will want you to return a puppy or dog to them if for some reason you are unable to continue to care for it, rather than seeing the dog go to a shelter or rescue facility.

If the breeder you are considering does not offer this type of return policy, find one who does, because no ethical breeder would ever permit a puppy from one of his or her litters to end up in a shelter.

d) Return Contract: reputable breeders offer return contracts. They do this to protect their reputation and to also make sure that a puppy they have sold that might display a genetic defect will not have the opportunity to breed and continue to spread the defect, which could weaken the entire breed.

Many breeders also offer return contracts because purchasing a puppy from a breeder can be an expensive proposition, and if you find out that the puppy has a worrisome genetic defect, this could cost you a great deal with respect to unexpected veterinarian care. In such cases, most honest and reputable breeders offer a return policy, and will be happy to give you another puppy.

e) Testimonials: ask the breeder you are considering to provide you with testimonials from some of their previous clients, and then actually contact those people to ask them about their experience with the breeder, and the health and temperament of their dog. A good breeder has nothing to hide and will be more than happy to provide you with testimonials because their best recommendation is a happy customer.

f) Breeder Reputation: the Internet can be a valuable resource when researching the reputation of a breeder. For instance, you will be able to post on most forums discussing breeders to quickly find out what you need to know from those who have firsthand experience.

Be prepared to answer questions the breeder may have for you, because a reputable breeder will want to ask a prospective purchaser their own questions, so that they can satisfy themselves that you are going to be a good caretaker for their puppy.

First do your homework about the breed you are considering and then carry out as much research as possible about the specific breeder you are considering before making your initial visit to their facility.

The more information you have gathered about the breed, and the breeder you are considering, and the more information the breeder knows about you, the more successful the match will be.

Chapter 4: Vital Statistics

1. Country of Origin

The United States is believed to be the country of origin for the Miniature Golden Retriever and although they may be some controversy over the topic of who was the first to create the Mini Golden, some believe that Kathy Burgess, who trademarked the name *"Comfort Retriever",* was the first.

2. Litter Size

While more or less can be born, an average litter size will be between 6 and 8 puppies.

3. Height and Weight

When measured at the shoulder, the Miniature Golden Retriever may stand between 14 and 20 inches (35.5 and 50.8 centimeters) and weigh between 20 and 45 pounds (9.07 and 20.41 kilograms) or more, depending on the size of both parents.

Keep in mind that puppies who inherit a higher proportion of the larger Golden Retriever genetics will likely grow to be larger dogs, while those that have more Poodle genes will probably be smaller.

Generally speaking, smaller dogs tend to live longer than larger ones.

4. Temperature & Heart Rate

Temperature: 100.5 to 102.5 degrees Fahrenheit (38.05 to 39.16 Celsius).

Respiratory Rate: 10 to 20 per minute

Pulse: Puppies, 120 to 160 per minute. Adults, 60 to 140 per minute.

Gums: should be pink

5. Lifespan

Depending on their size and health, the average Miniature Golden Retriever lifespan will be approximately 10 to 15 years, with some living even longer.

6. Coat Colors and Features

While the Golden Retriever is usually quite a heavy shedder, and most breeders will claim that the Miniature Golden Retriever double coat sheds less, the resulting puppies can be any combination of the straight Golden or Cocker or wavy, curly and soft texture inherited from the Poodle side of this mix.

Keep in mind that it may be a difficult task to predict how much less your Mini Golden may shed because this can vary considerably as each offspring will each inherit different characteristics from each parent involved in the breeding program.

Standard coat colors for the Miniature Golden Retriever may be cream through golden and red with some white on the chest, and you will need to regularly groom this dog to keep it looking healthy.

Eyes – will be medium-sized, oval-shaped and usually dark or hazel in color, with a soft and friendly expression.

Ears – will be long and pendant with rounded tips.

Tail – will be usually be long and heavily plumed and carried in a gay waving flag.

Adult Coats: the adult coat will begin to grow in at approximately 9-months of age. The entire process and complete change over to the adult coat will usually take 3 or 4 months or longer to fully complete.

During this time of coat change over, it will be very important to thoroughly brush or rake out your young dog's coat every day to help remove dead hair, mats and tangles, while the new coat grows in and they will require brushing every few days to keep them looking their best.

Defining Features: the most distinctive features of the Miniature Golden Retriever breed are their friendly and alert temperament and soft expression and that most of them will look remarkably like a smaller version of a Golden Retriever.

7. Intelligence

Stanley Coren, a professor of psychology at the University of British Columbia, in Vancouver, B.C., Canada, published ***The Intelligence of Dogs*** in 1994. Since then this book has become the standard for rating the particular intelligence of different canine breeds.

Coren's book describes three categories of dog intelligence:

(1) *Instinctive intelligence*;

(2) *Adaptive intelligence*, and

(3) *Working and obedience intelligence.*

He writes *"Instinctive intelligence refers to a dog's ability to carry out tasks it was bred to perform, such as guarding, herding, hunting, pointing, retrieving, or supplying companionship."* Coren further notes that:

> *"Adaptive intelligence refers to how well a dog is able to solve problems on its own"* and that *"Working and obedience intelligence refers to how quickly a dog is able to learn from humans."*

While Stanley Coren does not rank the Miniature Golden Retriever, as they are a combination of 2 or 3 highly intelligent canines that were all originally gun dogs, both the Golden Retriever and Poodle ranking #4 and #2 out of a possible 79, in the *"Brightest Dogs"* category, which means that these dogs can understand new commands after fewer than 5 repetitions and will obey first commands 95% of the time, or better and the Cocker Spaniel ranks #24 in the "Excellent Working Dogs" category (understanding new commands after between 5 and 15 repetitions and obeying first commands 85% of the time or better), all of which means that there is no question that the Mini Golden will be an exceptionally intelligent dog.

Please keep in mind that there are always exceptions to every study and a particular breed's degree of intelligence can often be related to their early upbringing and how they are trained.

No matter how intelligent a particular Miniature Golden may or may not be, there is no doubt that this energetic dog will be an alert, loyal, friendly and happy companion that will enjoy learning new things and as much activity as their guardian can provide.

8. Living Conditions

The Miniature Golden Retriever may be better suited to smaller living conditions, such as an apartment, than the standard sized Golden Retriever. However, ideally, this medium-sized, energetic dog would do best in a home with a large, securely fenced back yard or access to property where they can freely exercise.

This hybrid has been specifically bred to suit owners who may be unable or unwilling to manage the size and care requirements necessary with the larger, standard Golden Retriever but still want a dog that retains the friendly qualities and happy disposition of the Golden breed.

Although requiring less food and usually shedding less than the standard Golden, this more manageable companion sized dog still needs plenty of regular exercise and needs the space to regularly run and play.

This intelligent dog may become bored, destructive and unhappy unless you have a way to keep them both mentally and physically exercised outside of the home, which will include providing them with a moderate to high amount of disciplined walks and plenty of daily exercise or canine sports in order to maintain a happy disposition and a healthy weight.

A fully grown Miniature Golden Retriever will need to burn off their daily pent-up energy by going for at least three good walks of 30 minutes to an hour every day plus the opportunity to run freely with other dogs, swim or play fetch or be involved in a canine sport so that this highly intelligent, dog will be happy and well balanced.

Dogs are pack animals, which means that it is not normal for them to be by themselves. Therefore, leaving them alone for many hours every day with nothing for them to do, will be torture for them that could result in any dog becoming depressed or unhappy or making his or her own entertainment by becoming destructive, extremely noisy or attempting to escape so they can wander the neighborhood.

Chapter 5: Temperament

As a puppy, the Miniature Golden Retriever will be loving and playful and will bond closely with their family.

As an adult dog they will usually be happy to greet strangers and new people in a friendly manner because a well-bred dog will take on the friendly character and calm temperament of the Golden Retriever.

This smaller dog will be a happy family pet that will love plenty of attention and play and daily exercise in many forms and they will be eager and quick to learn students.

No matter how friendly your Mini Golden might be, it will always be imperative to properly socialize them, and when you put in the effort and considerable time involved in doing so, beginning at an early age and continuing throughout their life, they will be a wonderful companion.

When you do take the time you will help to ensure that your puppy grows up to be a sensible and calm adult dog that will take their cues from you, rather than having to make human decisions and act on their own.

This breed will become very attached and devoted to its family members and if you neglect this dog and do not provide them with regular daily exercise and mental stimulation, they may create their own entertainment through destructive behavior.

The Miniature Golden Retriever will be a loving family dog that is affectionate and totally devoted to the family.

1. Behavior With Children and Pets

The Miniature Golden Retriever will generally be friendly to all and loyal, affectionate and playful with children.

The Mini Golden will also be accepting and friendly with all other pets in their family, and while not a good guard dog, they will definitely be a dog that will bark to let you know when strangers or visitors are arriving at your door.

2. Is This Dog an Escape Artist?

The Miniature Golden Retriever is highly loving, incredibly intelligent and devoted to their family and when you combine their intelligence with their athletic ability, and the fact that they will get bored without something interesting to do, this makes them a talented escape artist.

They can certainly figure out how to escape from confinement will use their strong legs to jump fences, climb fences, dig under fences or find cracks they can squeeze through if they want to get out, and they usually will want to get out because they always want to engaged in interesting pursuits with their family and if they are left at home alone, they may well seek adventure and companionship elsewhere.

Of course, all dogs will have a much higher urge to roam before they are spayed or neutered, therefore, early spaying or neutering of a puppy will go a long way toward helping to curb any wanderlust tendencies that may be a result of raging hormones.

Chapter 6: Before You Buy

No matter what breed or combination of breed you may be considering as a possible candidate for sharing your home and life, this decision should never be entered into lightly.

As with any breed, those who may be considering a Miniature Golden Retriever need to carry out research and make sure they have all the facts straight before taking the plunge because there are always many important factors to keep in mind.

1. Miniature Golden Retriever Quick Review

The following is a quick review of the top categories to carefully consider before choosing a Miniature Golden Retriever as your canine companion.

Overall Temperament: Excellent
Friendliness with Family: Excellent
Friendliness with Strangers: Excellent
Suitability for City or Urban Living: Good
Suitability for Country or Rural Living: Excellent
Prey Drive: Variable
Guarding Capabilities: Poor
Watch Dog Capabilities: Excellent
Canine Sports – Agility, Obedience, Trick Training: Excellent
Grooming Requirements: Moderate
Hypoallergenic: Possibly
Exercise Requirements: Medium to High

Probably the most important consideration when researching a particular breed of dog to share your life with is your activity level and the exercise requirements of the breed you are considering.

2. Pros of Miniature Golden Retriever Ownership

The Miniature Golden Retriever has many good qualities to consider, including:

- Loyal, intelligent and loving;
- Excellent watchdog;

- Eager to learn and easy to train;
- Excellent candidate for any number of canine sports;
- Friendly and good with children, pets and people;
- May be a good choice for active first time dog guardians.

2. Cons of Miniature Golden Retriever Ownership

No matter what breed you choose, there will always be some downsides to carefully consider, including:

- A moderate to highly active, medium sized dog that loves plenty of activity to keep them both physically and mentally healthy;
- They may be talented escape artists;
- Easily bored – can lead to destructive behavior, barking or escape attempts;
- This dog needs an active owner that has lots of time to spend with them each day;
- This dog needs plenty of daily attention, ongoing training and socializing and the opportunity to be involved in canine sports.

IF I were considering sharing my life with a Miniature Golden Retriever, I would need to carefully and honestly answer the following questions:

a) Am I fit and active enough to be able to provide this highly intelligent and active companion with the correct amount of daily exercise and mental stimulation they need to be healthy and mentally stable? This means that I must have enough time in my day to involve them in activities beyond daily walks that will engage their intelligent minds.

b) Do I fully understand that this intelligent dog absolutely needs a high degree of daily mental stimulation, and physical and mental challenges so that they do not become bored and unhappy?

c) Am I able to spend the time to properly train, socialize and provide this dog with the appropriate rules and boundaries it needs to remain a calm follower and happy family member?

d) Am I aware that without the proper training, plenty of mental stimulation and ongoing exercise that exercises their brilliant mind, such as a canine sport (Agility, Flyball, Frisbee, Dock Diving,

Trick Training, Advanced Obedience, etc.) that this highly intelligent dog will gain weight, leading to poor health, and you may also be faced with behavioral problems?

e) Am I aware that while this dog can do well in a smaller environment (such as an apartment), so long as you get them outside several times every day to get plenty of running exercise, that ideally they would do best in a home with a back yard where they can safely play and run off leash?

If you can honestly answer YES to the above list of questions, then the Miniature Golden Retriever may be the dog for you.

Chapter 7: Choosing the Right Dog

1. US Clubs, Registries & Breeders

When wondering where to begin your search for purchasing a Miniature Golden Retriever puppy in the United States, a good starting point will be to first check local clubs and registries.

Before choosing, please keep in mind that every dog is different — don't get this dog (or any dog, for that matter) because you had one before that was a sweetheart everybody loved. The reality of the situation is that the next Miniature Golden Retriever will more than likely be totally different.

This is a relatively new hybrid canine creation, which also means that this companion dog comes with quite a high price tag. Also, there is no official online club yet established in the United States.

Adopt a Pet (online): *"…is North America's largest non-profit pet adoption website. We help over 13,600 animal shelters, humane societies, SPCAs, pet rescue groups, and pet adoption agencies advertise their homeless pets to millions of adopters a month, for free. We're all about getting homeless pets into homes…"*

Comfort Retrievers (in Kentucky): *"…Being a lover of Golden Retrievers for many years is what got us into breeding. Through our years of breeding we have had many people tell us that they wanted a golden retriever, but found the breed a bit too large for them.*

We had the idea for years of creating a hybrid dog that looked and acted like a golden retriever but in a smaller, more comfortable size. We envisioned a dog that looked like a miniature, small or petite golden retriever, and through our vision we created the Comfort Retriever®…"

Miniature Golden Retriever (in Montana): **"…***We are a FAMILY breeder and all of our dogs are indoor/outdoor pets. Temperament is a KEY factor in our breeding program. We have been raising miniature golden retrievers since about 2005. During that time, we have placed MANY happy puppies with happy owners. We have had less than 1% of health or temperament issues of any kind ever…"*

2. UK Clubs, Registries & Breeders

The Kennel Club is a registration and information service to help prospective owners find Kennel Club “assured breeders” of both purebreds and cross breeds.

This is a relatively new, North American hybrid canine creation and as such there is no official online club yet established in the United Kingdom.

As the Miniature Golden Retriever has been created in the United States, there is currently no online breeder to be found in the United Kingdom. If you are interested in this hybrid canine, the first step might be to contact a Goldendoodle (Golden Retriever/Poodle cross) in your area.

3. Average Prices for Puppies

There is a wide range of *“average”* pricing for any purebred Miniature Golden Retriever, depending upon the mix, the reputation of the breeder and whether you want a show quality dog or simply a companion, with some adoptions or rescues beginning around $300 (£179).

Although you may find puppies for sale that cost less or more, average prices from reputable breeders will range between $1,500 and $4,000 (£1,104 and £2,946), depending on the size of the puppies, whether they are of show or companion or working quality and the expertise of the particular breeder.

Important Note: the authors of this book have not purchased dogs from all the breeders mentioned in this book, and we do not recommend any particular breeder. Make sure that you thoroughly carry out your own research before purchasing a dog from any breeder. There are many dog breeders trading purely for profit and these often will not be overly concerned about the well being of the dogs they breed.

4. Avoiding Puppy Mills or Farms

As soon as a particular breed of dog becomes popular, they also become particularly susceptible to being bred by disreputable, high profit *“puppy mills”* or *“commercial breeding farms”*.

Often a specific dog breed will quickly gain popularity due to the *“Lassie”* effect, which occurs when a dog is featured in a popular movie.

Puppy Mill breeding is especially prevalent with cute, smaller breeds, as it takes less space to mass-produce smaller dogs.

This inhumane and cruel world of canine pregnancy for profit occurs all over the world, and if you are not very careful about where and how you purchase your Miniature Golden Retriever puppy, you may unknowingly end up promoting this disreputable practice.

Not only do Puppy Mills seriously contribute to overpopulation, they produce diseases and genetically flawed puppies that may suffer greatly with behavioral and/or health related problems that will cost their guardians greatly in terms grief and stress and the unexpected financial burden associated with veterinarian and behavioral costs, while the puppy's life may be cut prematurely short.

These dogs suffer in ways most of us could never imagine. For instance, most of these poor breeding dogs have never walked on solid ground or felt grass as they are housed in cramped wire cages. Females are bred continuously until they can no longer produce puppies, at which time they are sold to laboratories for experiments, killed or dumped on the side of a road.

Although the puppy mill problem is certainly not exclusive to the United States, as it happens all over the world, the problem is so rampant in the US that several states are actually labeled as "Puppy Mill States". These include Missouri, Nebraska, Kansas, Iowa, Arkansas, Oklahoma and Pennsylvania.

It can be difficult to shut down these mill or mass-producing farming operations because, just like the drug trade, it is business on a large and lucrative scale.

Although Puppy Mill puppies are sold in a variety of different venues, pet stores are the main source for selling these unfortunate puppies, who are taken away from their mothers far too young (at 4 to 5 weeks of age) and sold to brokers, who pack them into crates to ship them off to pet stores. Many innocent puppies die during transportation.

Think seriously before buying a puppy from a pet store because almost all puppies found in pet stores (whether or not the employees working there are aware of it) are the result of inhumane puppy mill breeding. If you purchase one of these puppies, you are helping to enable and perpetuate

Cocko – nipping/biting.

this horribly cruel breeding practice.

Every time someone buys a puppy from a pet store, the store will order more from the Puppy Mill. As far as the pet store is concerned, the puppies are simply inventory, like bags of dog food, and when one item drops off of the inventory list, another is purchased to replace it.

Puppy Mill puppies are also sold at flea markets, on the side of the road, at the beach, through newspaper ads and through fancy websites and Internet classifieds.

The only way to put these shameful, commercial businesses out of business is by spreading the word and never buying a puppy from a pet store, or any other advertising medium, unless you have first thoroughly checked them out by visiting the facility in person.

Always be wary if you answer an advertisement for a low priced puppy for sale and the person selling offers to deliver the puppy to you, because this could easily be the first sign that you are about to be involved in an illegal Puppy Mill operation.

Educate yourself and spread the word to others about Puppy Mills, because this is the first step toward ensuring that yourself and everyone you know are never unknowingly involved in the suffering that is forced upon the breeding dogs and puppies trapped in a puppy mill or mass farming operation.

5. How to Choose the Right Puppy

Choosing the right puppy for your family and your lifestyle is more important than you might imagine. Many people do not give serious enough thought to sharing their home with a new puppy before they actually bring one home.

For instance, many of us choose a puppy solely based on what it looks like, because the breed may currently be popular, because they saw one in a TV movie, or because their family had the same kind of dog when they were growing up. None of these are good reasons.

a) Important Questions: in order to be fair to ourselves, our family and the puppy we choose to share our lives with, we humans need to take a serious look at our life, both as it is today and what we envision it being in the next ten to fifteen years, and then ask ourselves a few important, personal questions, and honestly answer them before making the commitment to a puppy, including:

1) Do I have the time and patience necessary to devote to a puppy, which will grow into a dog who needs a great deal of attention, training and endless amounts of my devotion?

2) Do I lead a physically active, medium or low intensity life? For instance, am I out jogging the streets daily or climbing mountains or would I rather spend my leisure time on the couch?

3) Do I like to travel a lot? Perhaps a dog small enough to travel in the plane cabin with me is a consideration.

4) Am I a neat freak or do I have allergies? A low or non-shedding breed might make more sense.

5) Do I have a young, growing family that takes up all my spare time and are my children old enough to carefully handle a puppy? A dog needs a lot of time and attention.

6) Am I physically fit and healthy enough to be out there walking a dog two to three times a day, every day, rain or shine (and much more when it's just a puppy or a highly active breed)?

7) Can I afford the food costs and the veterinarian expenses that are part of being a conscientious dog guardian?

8) Is the decision to bring a puppy into my life a family decision, or just for the children, who will quickly lose interest?

9) Have I thoroughly researched the breed I'm interested in, and is it truly compatible with my lifestyle or am I considering this breed because I had a similar dog when I was a child, or just because I like the way it looks?

10) What is the number one reason why I want a dog in my life?

Once you ask yourself these important questions and honestly answer them, you will have a much better understanding of the type of puppy that would be best suited for you and your family, and whether or not it should be a Miniature Golden Retriever.

If you are too busy for a dog, or choose the wrong dog that is not compatible with you or your family's energy and lifestyle, you will inevitably end up with an unhappy dog, which will lead to behavioral issues, which then will lead to an unhappy family and extra expenses to hire a professional to help you reverse unwanted behavioral problems.

Please take the time to choose wisely. If you have absolutely decided that the Miniature Golden Retriever is the right dog for you, the following tips will help you to choose the right puppy from the litter.

b) Careful Puppy Selection: although your breeder can often help you with selecting the right puppy for you and your family, you will likely be feeling especially drawn to one puppy over another.

Although there are other considerations, how you feel toward a particular puppy in a litter is also an important part of deciding which pup to bring home.

Beyond your feelings, considering other factors will help improve the odds of you having a positive guardianship experience with your new Miniature Golden Retriever puppy. For instance, being a little objective when evaluating each puppy in the litter will help you to make the right choice.

While some people become very emotional when choosing a puppy and will be attracted to those who display extremes in behavior because they want to *"save"* them, it is not a particularly good idea to choose a puppy that may be very shy or frightened in the hope that they may grow into a happy, well-behaved dog.

Some people will delve even further into their emotional desires or needs to *"save"* or *"rescue"* and will choose a particular puppy <u>because</u> it has obvious health or behavioral issues, and because they want to provide it with a chance that they believe the puppy might not otherwise have.

While it is certainly wonderful that we humans have the capacity to raise and care for puppies that may be afflicted with health or behavior problems, it's important that these types of decisions are not undertaken lightly, as such challenges can lead you down a path that could be an emotional roller coaster of highs and lows that can cause problems for both canine and human alike.

While many minor behavioral problems can be modified with early training, it's important to be aware that the time and effort needed to do so will be difficult to predict and you should be aware that *"rescuing"* a dog that could grow up to have behavioral problems may require the services of a professional dog whisperer or psychologist.

c) Pick of the Litter: generally speaking, when choosing a puppy out of a litter, look for one that is friendly and outgoing, rather than one who is overly aggressive or fearful.

Taking note of a puppy's social skills when they are still with their litter mates will help you to choose the right puppy to take home because puppies who demonstrate good social skills with their litter mates are much more likely to develop into easy going, happy adults who play well with other dogs.

In a social setting where all the puppies can be observed together, there are several important observations you can make, including:

(1) When the puppies are playing, notice which puppies are comfortable both on top and on the bottom when play fighting and wresting with their littermates, and which puppies seem to only like being on top. Puppies who don't mind being on the bottom or who appear to be fine with either position will usually play well with other dogs when they become adults.

(2) If the puppies have toys to play with, observe which puppies try to keep the toys away from the other puppies and which puppies share. Those who want to hoard the toys and keep all other puppies away may be more aggressive with other dogs over food or treats, or in play where toys are involved as they become older.

(3) Notice which puppies seem to like the company of the other pups and which ones seem to be loners. Puppies who like the company of their littermates are more likely to be interested in the company of other dogs as they mature than anti-social puppies.

(4) Observe the reaction of puppies that get yelped at when they bite or roughhouse with another puppy too hard. Puppies who ease up when another puppy yelps or cries are more likely to respond appropriately when they play too roughly as adults.

(5) In addition, check to see if the puppy you are interested in is sociable with people, because if they will not come to you, or display fear to strangers, this may be a problem when they become adults.

(6) Furthermore, always check if the puppy you are interested in is relaxed about being handled, because if they are not, they may become difficult with adults and children during daily interactions, during grooming or visits to the veterinarian's office.

6. How to Check If a Puppy is Healthy

Of course you will want to check if a puppy you are considering taking home is not just emotionally healthy, but also physically healthy.

First, ask to see veterinarian reports from the breeder to satisfy yourself that the puppy is as healthy as possible, and then once you make your decision to share your life with a particular puppy, make an appointment with your own veterinarian for a complete examination.

Before you get to this stage, however, there are a few general signs of good health to be aware of when choosing a healthy puppy from a litter, including the following:

- **Breathing** – a healthy puppy will breathe quietly, without coughing or sneezing, and there will be no crusting or discharge around their nostrils;
- **Body** – they will look round and well fed, with an obvious layer of fat over their rib cage;
- **Coat** – a healthy puppy will have a soft coat with no dandruff, dullness, greasiness or bald spots;
- **Energy** – a well-rested puppy will be alert and energetic;
- **Hearing** – a healthy puppy with good hearing should react if you clap your hands behind their head;
- **Genitals** – a healthy puppy will not have any sort of discharge visible in or around their genital or anal regions;
- **Mobility** – a healthy puppy will walk and run normally without wobbling, limping or seeming to be weak, stiff or sore; and
- **Vision** – a healthy puppy will have bright, clear eyes without crust or discharge and they should notice if a ball is rolled past them within their field of vision.

7. One Miniature Golden Retriever or Two?

While getting two Miniature Golden Retriever puppies at once will be twice the fun, it will also be twice the work, which means that you will need to be doubly alert and patient, and perhaps also lose even more sleep than you bargained for during the potty training phase.

Every puppy needs your constant attention and guidance, therefore, before taking the plunge, ask yourself if you have the time and energy to provide constant attention and guidance for two little puppies that could be running in opposite directions?

Many humans decide to get two puppies because they want their puppy to have someone to play with. Be careful that one of the reasons for this decision is not based on the fact that the human making this decision might not be the ideal candidate for having one puppy, let alone two.

For instance, if the reason you are considering two puppies is so that the one puppy will not be alone all day while you are at work, stop right there, because leaving one, two or a dozen puppies alone all day while you are at work is a terrible decision.

If this is your situation, you should NOT be considering any puppy at this stage of your life, and especially not one as loving and connected to their guardians as a Miniature Golden Retriever who will suffer severely by being left alone.

Another consideration when thinking about whether or not to get two puppies is that often when they grow up, there may be continual sibling rivalry as each puppy vies for your attention.

It is entirely possible that when the puppies mature, they will no longer get along with each other as well as they once did when they were young puppies, especially if both are the same sex.

Furthermore, when you have two puppies growing up together, one will always be the more dominant personality that will take over the other, and this could mean that neither puppy will fully develop their individual personalities. As well, when you have two puppies or dogs in your life, they generally tend to be less affectionate or interested in their human guardians as they have each other in their own pack of dogs to rely upon. This can mean that they will focus so much on each other that they will bond much less with you, which can make it more difficult to train or convince either that you are the actual leader of the pack.

Each puppy will require our individual attention when it comes time for training, and having two puppies in the picture can make it very difficult for them to concentrate or focus on the job at hand.

For instance, when you are teaching puppy #1 to "Sit" while puppy #2 is trying to bite the tail of puppy #l, your job is going to be much more challenging.

Most professional trainers or psychologists will advise that if you want two puppies, not to get them at the exact same time from the same litter, so that you have the opportunity to house train and teach basic commands to one puppy before you bring another one into the home.

8. The Best Age to Purchase a Puppy

Generally speaking, no puppy, including a Miniature Golden Retriever puppy, should be removed from their mother any earlier than 8 weeks of age and leaving them until they are **10 to 16 weeks of age is preferred** because this will give them the extra time to learn important life skills from the mother dog, including eating solid food and grooming.

As well, leaving a puppy amongst their littermates for a longer period of time will help to ensure that they learn socialization skills. Removing a puppy from the mother and other siblings too early could mean that they will miss out on valuable skills and may not socialize well with others.

For the first month of a puppy's life they will be on a mother's milk only diet. Once the puppy's teeth begin to appear, they will start to be weaned from mother's milk and by the age of 8 weeks should be completely weaned and eating just puppy food.

Removing a puppy from their mother any earlier than eight weeks could mean they are not fully weaned and they would be much more difficult to feed.

9. Should I Get a Male or Female?

Everyone you ask will have a personal opinion about whether you should get a male or a female of any breed. While you will find just as many humans preferring a male Miniature Golden Retriever over a female, if you are a first time dog guardian there may be a few considerations that can help you to make a more informed decision.

For instance, male dogs tend to want to mark or pee on anything upright (trees, telephone poles, tall grass, a stranger's leg) wherever they are out walking much more than females, however, a dominant female will also pee in an attempt to mark territory.

A male Miniature Golden Retriever, even a housebroken one, may try to lift their leg on furniture when visiting a home where there are other dogs present. When spaying and neutering your dog, the operation is much more invasive when spaying a female than the neutering process required for males.

Some humans pick their dogs based on sex alone because they cannot stop themselves from attributing human characteristics to their chosen dogs, and therefore believe that, for instance, a female dog will have a *"sweeter"* temperament, or a male dog may be more *"independent"*.

Of course, this is complete nonsense, because a dog is a dog, and it can be harmful to your relationship to project human emotions onto them or imagine that they will act like humans just because we are human.

Therefore, the best way to choose your puppy will be to take your time observing the litter when you visit the breeder.

10. The Miniature Golden Retriever Shopping List

Before bringing home your new puppy or dog for the first time, there will be a list of items you need to make sure you have on hand, including:

Food – usually the puppy will remain on whatever food they have been fed at the breeder's for at least the first couple of weeks, until they are well settled in their new home, so make sure you ask the breeder what brand to buy.

Food and Water Bowls – make sure they are small enough for a young Miniature Golden Retriever puppy to get close to so that they can easily eat and drink.

Kennel – when you buy your puppy's hard-sided kennel, make sure that you buy the size that will be appropriate for them when they are fully grown. It must be large enough so that (when fully grown) they can easily stand up and turn around inside it.

Martingale Collar, 2 Leashes and Harness – buy the harness and collar small enough to fit your puppy and buy new collars as they grow larger.

Leashes – you will be able to keep the same leashes as all you will ever need is a four foot (1.22 meters) leash made out of nylon webbing with a light weight clip at the end (do not buy a leash that has a heavy clip on the end as it will be difficult for your puppy to carry around).

Soft Beds – you will need one or two for comfortable sleeping when they are not in their kennel. Make sure that you buy the beds large enough for a full-grown Miniature Golden Retriever.

Canine Shampoo and Conditioner – always choose products that are the correct pH for a dog (never use human products). You will also need a non-slip mat for the sink or bathtub and lots of drying towels.

Finger Tooth Brush –- this is a soft, rubber cap that fits over the human's finger to get the puppy used to having their teeth regularly brushed, then a regular or electric toothbrush (an Oral-B electric is best).

Soft Bristle Brush or Comb for longer coats – for daily grooming.

Puppy Nail Scissors – for trimming their toenails, and a small, medium or large-sized pair of plier style nail clippers for when they are full grown.

One or two Soft Toys – or wait until they come home and let them pick their own toys from the store.

Daily Essentials – Pee Pads, Puppy sized Treats, Poop Bags.

Be sure to take your Miniature Golden Retriever shopping list with you when you go to your local pet store or boutique, otherwise you may forget critical items.

NOTE: if you do not already have a hairdryer, you will need to get one of these, too, so you can dry your puppy after bath time.

11. Puppy Proofing Your Home

Most puppies will be a curious bundle of energy, eager to explore everything, which means that they will get into everything within their

reach.
As a responsible puppy guardian, you will want to provide a safe environment for them, which means eliminating all sources of danger, similar to what you would do for a curious toddler.

Be aware that your puppy will want to touch, sniff, taste, chew, investigate and closely inspect every electrical cord, every closet, every nook and cranny of your home and everything you may have left lying about on the floor.

Power cords can be found in just about every room in the home and to a teething puppy, these may look like irresistible, fun chew toys. Make sure that you tuck all power cords securely out of your puppy's reach or enclose them inside a chew-proof PVC tube.

Kitchen – first of all, there are many human foods that can be harmful to dogs, therefore, your kitchen should always be strictly off limits to your puppy any time you are preparing food. Calmly send them out of the kitchen any time you are in the kitchen, and they will quickly get the idea that this area is off limits to them.

Bathroom – bathroom cupboards and drawers or the side of a bathtub where you may leave your shaving supplies can hold many dangers for a young and curious puppy. Kleenex, cotton swabs, Q-tips, toilet paper, razors, pills, soap or other materials left within your puppy's reach are an easy target that could result in an emergency visit to your veterinarian's office. Family members need to put shampoos, soap, facial products, makeup and accessories out of reach or safely inside a cabinet or drawer.

Bedroom – if you don't keep your shoes, slippers and clothing safely behind doors, you may find that your puppy has claimed them for their new chew toys. Be vigilant about keeping everything in its safe place, including jewelry, hair ties, bills, coins, and other items small enough for them to swallow in containers or drawers, and secure any exposed cords or wires. If you have children, make sure they understand that, especially while your puppy is going through their teething stage, they must keep their rooms picked up and leave nothing that could cause a choking problem to the puppy lying about on the floor or within their reach.
Living Room – we humans spend many hours in our cozy gathering places to watch movies or play games, and often the living areas of our homes will have many items that are very enticing for a curious and teething puppy, such as books, magazines, pillows, iPods, cell phones, TV remotes

and more. You will want to keep your home free of excess clutter and remain vigilant about straightening up and putting things out of sight that could be tempting to your puppy.

Office – we often spend a great deal of time in our home offices, which means that our puppy will want to be there, too, and they will be curious about all the items an office has to offer, such as cell phones, papers, books, magazines, and electrical cords. Although your puppy might think that rubber bands or paper clips are fun to play with, allowing these items to be within your puppy's reach could end up being a fatal mistake if your puppy swallows them.

Plants: – can be a very tempting target for your puppy's teeth, so you will want to keep them well out their reach. If you have floor plants, they will need to be moved to a shelf or counter or placed behind a closed door until your curious fur friend grows out of the habit of putting everything in their mouth. Also keep in mind that many common houseplants are poisonous to dogs (discussed in Chapter 15).

Garage and Yard – there are obvious as well as subtle dangers that could seriously harm or even kill a puppy, which can often be found in the garage or yard. Some of these might include antifreeze, gasoline, fertilizers, rat, mice, snail and slug poison, weed killer, paint, cleaners and solvents, grass seed, bark mulch and various insecticides.

If you are storing any of these toxic substances in your garage or garden shed, make certain that you keep all such products inside a locked cabinet, or stored on high shelves that your puppy will not be able to reach. Even better, choose not to use toxic chemicals anywhere in your home or yard.

12. Puppy Hazard Home Inspection

Every conscientious puppy guardian needs to take a serious look around the home not just from the human eye level, but also from the eye level of a Miniature Golden Retriever puppy.

This means literally crawling around your floors. This can be a fun exercise to ask your children to help you with.
Your puppy has a much lower vantage point than you do when standing, therefore, there may be items in your environment that could potentially be harmful to a puppy that a human might not notice unless you get down on the floor and take a really good look.

Remember that most dogs are food motivated, therefore they will put everything into their mouth and it will be up to you to ensure that they do not eat something that could harm them.

13. The First Weeks With Your Puppy

a) The First Night: before you go to the breeder's to pick up your new Miniature Golden Retriever puppy, vacuum your floors, including all the dust bunnies under the bed.

Do a last minute check of every room to make sure that everything that could be a puppy hazard is carefully tucked away out of sight and that nothing is left on the floor or low down on shelves where a curious puppy might get into trouble.

Close most of the doors inside your home, so that there are just one or two rooms that the puppy will have access to. You have already been shopping and have everything you need, so get out a puppy pee pad and have it at the ready when you bring your new furry friend home.

Also have your soft bed(s) in an area where you will be spending most of your time and where your puppy can easily find them. If you have already purchased a soft toy, take the toy with you when you go to pick up your puppy.

NOTE: take either your hard-sided kennel or your soft-sided "Sherpa" travel bag (lined with pee pads) with you when going to bring your new puppy home, and make sure that it is securely fastened to the seat of your vehicle with the seatbelt restraint system.

Even though you will be tempted to hold your new puppy in your lap on the drive home, this is a very dangerous place for them to be, in case of an accident. Place them inside their kennel or bag, which will be lined with soft towels and perhaps even a warm, towel-wrapped hot water bottle (and a pee pad), and close the door.

If you have a friend who can drive for you, sit beside your puppy in the back seat, and if they cry on the way home, remind them that they are not alone with your soft, soothing voice.

Before bringing your new puppy inside your home, take them to the place where you want them to relieve themselves and try to wait it out long enough for them to at least go pee. Then bring them inside your home and introduce them to the area where their food and water bowls will be kept, in case they are hungry or thirsty.

Let your puppy wander around sniffing and checking out their new surroundings and encourage them to follow you wherever you go. Show them where the puppy pee pad is located and place it near the door where you will exit to take them outside to go potty. Many pee pads are scented to encourage a puppy to pee, and if they do, happily praise them.

Show them where their hard-sided kennel is (in your bedroom) and put them inside with the door open while you sit on the floor in front of it and quietly encourage them to relax inside their kennel.

Depending on the time of day you bring your new puppy home for the first time, practice this kennel exercise several times throughout the day, and if they will take a little treat each time you encourage them to go inside their kennel, this will help to further encourage the behavior of them wanting to go inside.

After they have had their evening meal, take them outside approximately 20 minutes later to go to the bathroom, and when they do, make sure you are very enthusiastic with your praise and perhaps even give a little treat.

So far your puppy has only been allowed in several rooms of your home, as you have kept the other doors closed, so keep it this way for the first few days.

Before it's time for bed, again take your puppy outside for a very short walk to the same place where they last went potty and make sure that they go pee before bringing them back inside. Before bed, prepare your puppy's hot water bottle and wrap it in a towel so that it will not be too hot for them, and place it inside their hard-sided kennel (in your bedroom).

Turn the lights down low and invite your puppy to go inside their kennel and if they seem interested, perhaps give them a soft toy to have inside with them. Let them walk into the kennel under their own steam and when they do, give them a little treat (if they are interested) and encourage them to snuggle down to sleep while you are sitting on the floor in front of the kennel.
Once they have settled down inside their kennel, close the door, go to your bed and turn all the lights off. It may help your puppy to sleep during their

first night home if you can play quiet, soothing music in the background.

If they start to cry or whine, stay calm and have compassion because this is the first time in their young life when they do not have the comfort of their mother or their litter mates.

Do not let them out of their kennel if they are crying, but rather, simply reassure them with your calm voice that they are not alone until they fall asleep.

TIP

If your bed is wide enough to accommodate your puppy's kennel, it may help them to fall asleep for the first few nights in their new kennel if you have it beside you on top of the bed, so that you are closer to them. If there is any danger of the kennel falling off the bed during the night, do NOT do this as you will traumatize your puppy and make them afraid of their kennel.

b) The First Week: during the first week, you and your new Miniature Golden Retriever puppy will be getting settled into their new routine, which will involve you getting used to your puppy's needs as they also get used to your usual schedule.

Be as consistent as possible with your waking and sleeping routine, getting up and going to bed at the same time each day, so that it will be easier for your puppy to get into the flow and routine of their new life.

First thing in the morning, remove your puppy from their kennel and take them immediately outside to relieve themselves at the place where they last went pee.

At this time, if you are teaching them to ring a doorbell to go outside, let them ring the bell before you go out the door with them, whether you are carrying them, or whether they are walking out the door on their own.

NOTE: during the first week, you may want to carry your puppy outside first thing in the morning as they may not be able to hold it for very long once waking up.

When you bring them back inside, you can let them follow you so they get used to their new leash and/or harness arrangement. Be very careful not to drag your puppy if they stop or pull back on the leash.

TIP

If they refuse to walk on the leash, just hold the tension toward you (without pulling) while encouraging them to walk toward you, until they start to move forward again.

Now it will be time for their first feed of the day, and after they have finished eating, keep an eye on the clock, because you will want to take them outside to relieve themselves in about 20 minutes.

When your puppy is not eating or napping, they will be wanting to explore and have little play sessions with you and these times will help you bond with your puppy more and more each day.

As their new guardian, it will be your responsibility to keep a close eye on them throughout the day, so that you can notice when they need to relieve themselves and either take them to their pee pad or take them outside.

You will also need to make sure that they are eating and drinking enough throughout the day, so set regular feeding times at least three times a day. Also set specific times in the day when you will take your puppy out for a little walk on leash and harness, so that they are not only going outside when they need to relieve themselves, but they are also learning to explore their new neighborhood with you beside them.

When your puppy is still very young, you will not want to walk for a long time as they will get tired easily, and you do not want to stress joints or bones that are growing, so keep your walks to no more than 15 or 20 minutes during your first week and if they seem tired or cold, pick them up and carry them home.

14. Common Mistakes to Avoid

1) Sleeping in Your Bed: many people make the mistake of allowing a crying puppy to sleep with them in their bed, and while this may help to calm and comfort a new puppy, it will set a dangerous precedent that can result in behavioral problems later in their life.

In addition, a sleeping human body can easily crush a puppy.

As much as it may pull on your heart strings to hear your new puppy crying the first couple of nights in their kennel, a little tough love at the beginning will keep them safe while helping them to learn to both love and respect you as their leader.

2) Picking Them Up at the Wrong Time: never pick your puppy up if they display nervousness, fear or aggression (such as growling) toward an object, person or other pet, because this will be rewarding them for unbalanced behavior.

Instead, your puppy needs to be gently corrected by you, with firm and calm energy so that they learn not to react with fear or aggression.

3) Armpit Alligators: when your dog is a small size, be aware that many guardians get into the bad habit of carrying a small dog or puppy far too much. They need to be on the ground and walking on their own so that they do not become overly confident because a dog that is carried by their guardian is literally being placed in the *"top dog"* position.

Humans who constantly carry small dogs around rather than allowing them to walk on their own can often inadvertently create what I refer to as an *"armpit alligator"* situation.

While the Miniature Golden Retriever is usually friendly with everyone, without proper socialization it is possible to teach any dog be become intolerant of other people and pets, which means that it is always possible to allow them to become protective or possessive of *"their"* humans.

This happens when the dog becomes possessive of its guardian who carries it everywhere, and when another adult, child or dog sees the cute little dog and approaches to say hello, the cute little dog who has been inadvertently trained to believe that it is the boss may then lunge, snap and/or growl.

4) Playing Too Hard or Too Long: many humans play too hard or allow their children to play too long or too roughly with a young puppy. You need to remember that a young puppy tires very easily and especially during the critical growing phases of their young life, they need their rest.

5) Hand Play: always discourage your puppy from chewing or biting your hands, or any part of your body for that matter.

If you allow them to do this when they are puppies, they will want to continue to do so when they have strong jaws and adult teeth and this is not acceptable behavior for any breed of dog. Do not get into the habit of playing the *"hand"* game, where you rough up the puppy and slide them across the floor with your hands, because this will teach your puppy that your hands are playthings and you will have to work hard to break this bad habit.

When your puppy is teething, they will naturally want to chew on everything within reach, and this will include you. As cute as you might think it is, this is not an acceptable behavior and you need to gently, but firmly, discourage the habit.

A light flick with a finger on the end of a puppy nose, combined with a firm "NO" and removing the enticing fingers by making a fist when they are trying to bite human fingers will discourage them from this activity.

6) Not Getting Used to Grooming: not taking the time to get your Miniature Golden Retriever used to a regular grooming routine, including bathing, brushing, toenail clipping and teeth brushing can lead to a lifetime of trauma for both human and dog every time these procedures must be performed.

Set aside a few minutes each day for your grooming routine.

NOTE: get your Miniature Golden Retriever used to being up high, on a table or countertop when you are grooming them, because when it comes time for a full grooming session, or a visit to the vet's office where they will be placed on an examination table, then they will not be stressed by being placed in an unfamiliar situation.

7) Free Feeding: means to keep food in your puppy's bowl 24/7 so that they can eat any time of the day or night, whenever they feel like it.

While free feeding a young puppy can be a good idea (especially with very small dogs) until they are about four or five months old, many guardians often get into the bad habit of allowing their adult dogs to continue to eat food any time they want, by leaving food out 24/7.

Getting into this type of habit can be a serious mistake, as your dog needs to know that you are absolutely in control of their food. If your dog does not associate the food they eat with you, they may become picky eaters or think that they are in charge, which can lead to other behavioral issues later in life.

8) Treating Them Like Children: do not get into the bad habit of treating your dog like a small, furry human, because even though they may try their best to please you, and their doggy smarts could help them to succeed in most instances, not honoring them for the amazing dog they are will only cause them confusion that could lead to behavioral problems.

IMPORTANT: remember that the one thing your Miniature Golden Retriever is the absolute best at is being a dog.

A well-balanced dog thrives on rules and boundaries, and when they understand that there is no question that you are their leader and they are your follower, they will live a contented, happy and stress-free life.

9) Distraction and Replacement: when your puppy tries to chew on your hand, foot, clothing or anything else that is not fair game, you need to firmly and calmly tell them "No", and then distract them by replacing what they are not supposed to be chewing with their chew toy.

Make sure that you happily praise them every time they choose the toy to chew on. If the puppy persists in chewing on you, remove yourself from the equation by getting up and walking away.

If they are really persistent, put them inside their kennel with a favorite chew toy until they calm down.

Always praise your puppy when they stop inappropriate behavior or replace inappropriate behavior with something that is acceptable to you, so that they begin to understand what they can and cannot do.

15. Bonding With Your Dog

You will begin bonding with your puppy or dog from the very first moment you bring them home from the breeder.

This is the time when your puppy or dog will be the most upset and nervous, as they will no longer have the guidance, warmth and comfort of their mother or their other littermates, and you will need to take on the role of being your new fur friend's center of attention.

Be patient, kind and gentle with them as they are learning that you are now their new center of the universe.

Your daily interaction with your puppy during play sessions and especially your disciplined exercises, including going for walks on a leash, and teaching commands and tricks, will all be wonderful bonding opportunities.

Do not make the mistake of thinking that *"bonding"* with your new puppy can only happen if you are playing or cuddling together, because the very best bonding happens when you are kindly teaching rules and boundaries, and this intelligent puppy will be most eager to learn.

16. What Does the Wag Mean?

It can be a mistake to automatically assume that if a dog is wagging their tail that they are happy and friendly.

When determining a dog's true intent or demeanor, it's important to take into consideration the entire dog, rather than just the tail, because it is entirely possible that a dog can be wagging it's tail just before it decides to take an aggressive lunge toward you.

More important in determining the emotional state of a dog is the height or positioning of the their tail.

For instance, a tail that is held parallel to the dog's back usually suggests that the dog is feeling relaxed, whereas if the tail is held stiffly vertical, this usually means that the dog may be feeling aggressive or dominant.

A tail held much lower can mean that the dog is feeling stressed, afraid, submissive or unwell and if the tail is tucked underneath the dog's body, this is most often a sign that the dog is feeling stressed, fearful or threatened by another dog or person.

Paying attention to your dog's tail can help you to know when you need to step in and make some space between your dog and another, more dominant dog.

Of course, different breeds naturally carry their tails at different heights, so you will need to take this into consideration when studying your dog's tail so that you get used to their particular signals.

As well, the speed the tail is moving at will also give you an idea of the mental state of the dog because the speed of the wag usually indicates how excited a dog may be.

For instance, a slow, slightly swinging wag can often mean that the dog is tentative about greeting another dog, and this is more of a questioning type of wag, whereas a fast moving tail held high can mean that a dog is about to challenge or threaten another less dominant dog.

Interestingly, two veterinarians at the University of Bari and a neuroscientist at the University of Trieste, in Italy, published a paper in which their research outlined that dogs' tails wagged more to their right side when they had positive feelings about a person or situation, and more to the left side when they were feeling negative.

While certainly a dog's tail can help us humans to understand how our dogs might be feeling, there are many other factors to take into consideration when determining a dog's state of mind.

17. What Does the Bark Mean?

Of course, our dogs bark for a wide variety of reasons, and every dog is different, depending upon their natural breed tendencies and how they were raised, and this section discusses some of the more common reasons why a dog might be barking.

a) Communication: since the very first dog, they have communicated over long distances by howling to one another and when in closer proximity, barking to warn off other dogs approaching what they consider to be their territory or in excitement or happiness when greeting another member of the dog pack.

Now, our domesticated dogs have learned that barking for a wide variety of reasons, in a guard dog capacity to alert us to someone approaching the home, in anticipation of their favorite food, when they are afraid or frustrated, or to let us know they want to play is an effective way to get the attention of us humans because barking is a difficult noise to ignore.

b) Danger: of course, our canine companions will bark to alert us to what they believe might be a dangerous situation, but how do we learn to understand the difference between what our dogs perceive as danger and what is truly dangerous, or indeed teach our best friends the difference?

We want our dogs to tell us when there is real imminent danger and in this case, should the danger involve an unwanted intruder, we want them to bark loudly to possibly scare this threat away.

Unfortunately, many dogs are not quite as discerning as we humans might prefer, and as such they may end up barking during situations that we would consider inappropriate or just plain annoying.

When our dogs are barking for a reason we are not yet aware of, we need to calmly assess the situation rather than immediately becoming annoyed. We also need to remember that our dog's sense of smell, hearing and sometimes eyesight is far more acute than our own, so we need to give them an opportunity to tell us they just heard, saw or sensed something that they are worried or uncertain about.

Rather than ignoring our dogs (or yelling at them) when they are attempting to "tell" us that something is bothering them, even if we ourselves understand that the noise the dog just heard is only the neighbor pulling into their driveway, we need to calmly acknowledge the dog's concern by saying, *"OK, good boy"* or *"OK, good girl"* and then asking them to come to you. This way you have quietly and calmly let your dog know that the situation is nothing to be concerned about and you have asked them to move away from the target they are concerned about, which will usually stop the barking.

c) Attention: many dogs will learn to bark to get their owner's attention, just because they are bored or want to be taken outside for an interesting walk or a trip to the local park to chase a ball.

Our canine companions are very good at manipulating us in this way, and if we fall for it, we are setting up an annoying precedent that could plague us for the remainder of our relationship.

When a dog is barking to gain their guardian's attention, even if it is warranted because (in this example) it is certainly time to go out for a walk, we must not be immediately manipulated. Instead, we need to calmly ask our dog to do something for us, before leaping up and getting the leash to take our dog out.

After our dog has performed a calm and quiet task for us, such as sit and lie down, then we can decide to take our dog out for a walk.

In another example, often you will see a dog and their guardian at the local dog park playing fetch and when the human is not throwing that ball quickly enough to satisfy the dog's desire to run and fetch, the dog will be madly barking at the guardian.

Do not make the mistake of allowing your dog to manipulate you in this situation, because if you do, you will have created another bad habit that will very quickly become not just annoying to you, but also annoying to everyone else at the park.

Before throwing a ball or Frisbee for a dog that loves to retrieve, it is important to always ask the dog to sit and make eye contact with you.

Often the types of canines that are overly exuberant with chasing a ball or Frisbee have learned this barking behavior from their humans who allowed themselves to be literally at the beck and call of the dog, and they did this by throwing the ball every time the dog barked.

If you allow your dog to dictate to you when you will throw the ball, they will quickly learn that barking gets them their desired result, and you have just created an annoying, rude dog who is yelling at you in doggy language to do their bidding.

In this type of ball retrieving scenario, the dog has become ball *"obsessed"* and is no longer really paying attention to the guardian's commands, as they are solely focusing on where the ball is.

There are many situations in which a dog may bark to convey a certain message, such as letting you know when they need to go outside for potty, and of course, this is a good thing.

However, in all other situations where a dog is barking to demand attention or an object or food, this is when you need to ask them to do something for you, and then only if you want to give them what they are asking for, do you follow through.

Also, remember to stay calm when a dog is demanding attention because even negative attention can be rewarding for a dog that can then learn further habits that will not be particularly acceptable for the human side of the relationship.

d) Boredom or Separation Anxiety: many dogs, especially those who have not been properly trained or that have not been allowed to understand that they have rules and boundaries, and are treated like children, will bark loudly when left at home alone and they are bored or are feeling the anxiety of being alone.

Many times we humans believe that a dog is barking when being left alone because the dog is experiencing "separation anxiety", when in fact what the dog is really experiencing is the frustration of observing a member of the pack which they believe to be their follower (i.e. You) leaving them.

These dogs are loudly verbalizing this frustration and displeasure because, in the dog world, the pack follower does NOT leave the pack leader. In these cases, the humans really need the expert advice of a dog whisperer or dog psychologist to help turn the situation around and put the human guardian back in the driver's seat.

Breaking a dog of the habit of loud barking when they are left alone can be solved in two different ways. The most obvious being that you simply take your dog with you wherever you go, because after all, they are pack animals, and in order for them to be really happy and well balanced, they need the constant direction of their leader (which is supposed to be you).

The other, much more lengthy and often more time consuming way to solve a barking problem, involves hiring a professional to help assess why the problem has occurred and devise a plan that will work for your unique situation.

e) Fear or Pain: another reason our canine companions will bark is when they are very frightened or in pain and this is usually a type of bark that sounds quite different from all the others, often being a combination of a bark and a whine, or a yelping type of noise.

This is a bark that you will want to pay close attention to so that you can quickly respond and offer the dog assistance that they may need.

Whatever reason your dog may be barking, always remember that this is how they communicate and "tell" us that they want something or are concerned, afraid, nervous or unhappy about something, and as their guardians, we humans need to pay attention.

Chapter 8: Health Problems

When considering what sort of health problems a purebred dog may be prone to, you will need to consider the health problems associated with the particular breed and in this case, that means any health concerns that may affect the Golden Retriever, the Cocker Spaniel or the Poodle.

Generally speaking, while a Miniature Golden Retriever puppy will be susceptible to any type of health condition that affects either of their parents, many potential health conditions can be avoided when choosing your puppy from a reputable breeder.

While a healthy Miniature Golden Retriever may live to be 10 to 15 years or more, and with proper care they may not suffer from any of the below noted health concerns, it is prudent to list all concerns possibly associated with each part of this breed so that you have a clear understanding of problems that *"may"* affect your dog.

Golden Retriever Health Concerns:

1) Hemangiosarcoma: is a form of cancer affecting the lining of the blood vessels.

2) Osteosarcoma: is a type of malignant bone cancer, the cause of which is not known, found in this breed. While a tumor can develop in any bone, they often occur in bones bordering the shoulder and knee. The tumor becomes more painful as it grows outward, destroying the bone from the inside out.

This highly aggressive cancer causes lameness that may appear suddenly and progress rapidly over several weeks. Treatment requires an aggressive plan, such as radiation therapy or even amputation of the affected bone.

3) Lymphosarcoma: is a form of cancer occurring within the lymph nodes, liver, spleen and bone marrow.

4) Mast Cell Tumors: are another form of cancer originating from bone marrow and found within the connective tissues throughout the dog's body.

According to a health study carried out in 1998, 61.4% of the American

Golden Retriever population died from cancer related health issues. A similar study carried out by the UK Kennel Club during 2004 placed cancer related deaths at 38.8%.

5) Hip and Elbow Dysplasia: this is a common condition where the head of the dog's femur (thigh bone) fits incorrectly into the elbow or hip joint socket. Approximately $1/5^{th}$ of dogs not screened develop this condition.

6) Luxating Patella: this slipping kneecap condition is a common defect seen in many breeds, including the Golden Retriever, that may also be caused by accidentally falling or jumping from a height.

Often you will see a dog with this problem appear to be skipping down the road as they occasionally life one leg when the kneecap slips out of the patellar groove and the leg locks up. Surgery is the treatment option for this condition, although many dogs live a relatively normal life with this defect.

7) Osteochondritis: is a joint disorder that causes cracks to form in the cartilage and underlying bone and is caused by lack of blood flow to the cartilage, which then results in the bone dying and being absorbed by the dog's body. When this occurs the joint can no longer move freely and movement causes discomfort, pain and more damage.

Causes of Osteochondritis can be due to trauma, poor nutrition, genetics or improper or too strenuous exercising at an early age and can affect the shoulder, knee, elbow or hock joints. Diagnosis requires x-ray and restricted activity. In severe cases surgery will be required to remove the defective cartilage.

8) Panosteitis: is a condition affecting the long bones that can cause sudden lameness due to unexplained pain. This usually occurs when the dog is still growing, during 5 and 14 months of age and usually resolves itself as the dog grows.

9) Cataracts: (which are common in many breeds), is an eye condition where the lens becomes cloudy or milky, which would be like trying to see through a foggy window. This eye condition can appear from birth to 3 years of age and will usually lead to blindness.

10) Progressive Retinal Atrophy (PRA): causes degeneration of the retina, which is part of the eye. The retina is the part that senses visual information and sends it to the brain. Degeneration of this vital part of the eye eventually will lead to blindness and this disease usually appears between 3 and 5 years of age. A simple DNA test is available to determine (without waiting for symptoms to appear).

This disease usually appears between 3 and 5 years of age. A simple DNA test is available to determine (without waiting for symptoms to appear).

11) Corneal Dystrophy: is a change in the eye usually attributed to aging, causing fluid leakage that appears as a bluish color in the inner layer of the cornea.

12) Retinal Dysplasia: appears as streaks or dots in the retina of the dog's eye, which can lead to blindness.

The Golden Retriever can also suffer from glaucoma from increased fluid pressure in the eye, and eyelash problems, such as distichiasis and entropion, where eyelashes grow in an abnormal location or the eyelid turns inward causing the lashes to rub against the eyeball.

13) Cardiomyopathy: is a disease of the heart that causes that causes weakness in the muscle tissues and a subsequent enlarging of the heart.

14) Pulmonic Stenosis: is a congenital narrowing in the area of the pulmonary heart valve located between the pulmonary artery and the right ventricular chamber of the dog's heart. Narrowing in this area, which can occur within the valve itself, impairs normal blood flow through the artery. When this happens blood flow can be seriously interrupted which then leads to right-sided heart failure.

This condition may be first diagnosed when hearing a heart murmur under stethoscopic examination. Dogs displaying signs of heart failure are treated with diuretics.

15) Moist Dermatitis: usually caused by a dog licking, chewing or scratching an area of their skin. These irritated areas become warm to the touch and because of this are often referred to as *"hot spots"*. These are most commonly associated with flea allergies.

16) Lick Granuloma: the Golden Retriever can also suffer from this self-inflicted condition, which is caused when the dog continually licks their lower legs or paws. This problem is considered to be a result of boredom, anxiety or stress resulting from an active dog being left alone for long periods of time.

Many noted health conditions can be prevented when conscientious breeders carefully screen breeding stock so that hereditary or genetic health conditions will not be passed on to subsequent litters of puppies.

Poodle Health Concerns

While a healthy Poodle may live to be 10 to 15 years or more (depending on their size), and with proper care may not suffer from any of the below noted health concerns, it is prudent to list all concerns possibly associated with this breed, including:

1) Progressive Retinal Atrophy (PRA): can appear at 3-5 years old. A simple DNA test is available so you can find out at any time (without waiting for symptoms) whether your Miniature Poodle has inherited PRA, or not.

2) Cataracts: can appear from birth to 3 years old and usually lead to blindness. Cataracts appearing after age 3 are usually milder.

3) Other Eye Problems: Poodles can also suffer from tear duct disorders, corneal ulcers, eyelash abnormalities, retinal dysplasia, and glaucoma.

4) Otitis Externa: is an inflammation of the ear canal, which can become chronic, and causes discomfort, irritation and pain. Ear infections are common due to the long narrow ear canals, long ears and profuse hair growth in the ear canals.

5) Cushing's Disease: there are three forms of Cushing's Disease and most dogs suffer from the more common form, *"Pituitary Dependent PD"*, which is a slow growing form of cancer that is located in the pituitary gland.

6) Cancer: Poodles affected by cancer are often those which were not neutered or spayed. Therefore, if you do not require your poodle to remain sexually intact for breeding, it makes sense to have them neutered or spayed.

7) **Hypothyroidism:** is a condition resulting from an inadequate

production of thyroid hormone, which is treated with medication. Symptoms include lethargy, obesity, excessive hunger, and a coarse coat texture. Testing for thyroid malfunction is done through blood sample.

8) Dental Disease: smaller Poodles, because of their smaller jaw, are prone to dental disease, which can be prevented if you regularly brush their teeth.

9) Pancreatitis: is especially common in middle-aged, overweight Poodles who are pudgy around the middle because they are over-fed and/or do not get enough daily exercise. Never suddenly give these dogs a meal or a treat that has a very high fat content, because this is the most common trigger of a pancreatitis attack, which can be fatal.

10) Epilepsy: these seizures can occur in all three sizes of Poodle and the most common cause is idiopathic epilepsy, which is an inherited form of epilepsy. However, many factors can cause seizures and it is very important to have a Miniature Poodle diagnosed if seizures begin.

11) Mitral Valve Disease (MVD): is a degeneration of the mitral heart valve that can lead to heart failure. If a dog has this problem, the blood will flow back into the chamber, which can cause the chamber to enlarge, which then can cause other problems, including an irregular heartbeat, constricted windpipe, or flowing back into the lungs.

The first signs of mitral valve disease is a heart murmur, which can usually only be heard with a stethoscope. Symptoms include fainting, coughing, increased blood pressure, tiredness and reluctance to exercise. There is no cure and beyond replacing the valve, management involves various drug therapies to improve the dog's quality of life.

12) Hip Dysplasia: is a condition in which the head of the femur fits improperly into the hip joint socket. Factors, which have an influence on the hips, include nutrition, a dog's environment and the condition of the hips of its parents. Screening for hip dysplasia is recommended for breeding stock.

13) Legg-Calve-Perthes Disease: is a more serious, but less common disease of the hip joint – degeneration of the head of the femur, which causes severe pain and lameness.

14) Luxating Patella: this slipping or floating kneecap condition is a common defect seen in many smaller breeds, including the Miniature

Poodle, and may also be caused by accidentally falling or jumping from a height.
Usually the condition will present itself between the ages of 4 and 6 months.

Often you will see a dog with this problem appear to be skipping down the road as they occasionally lift one leg as the kneecap slips out of the patellar groove and the leg locks up. In more severe cases, surgery may be the recommended treatment option to correct this condition.

15) Tracheal Collapse: is a airway obstruction of the trachea, or "*windpipe*," sometimes also referred to as *"reverse sneezing"*. The trachea is a tube made up of sturdy rings of cartilage through which air is transported in and out of the dog's lungs.

As air is squeezed through the windpipe during breathing, sometimes the tracheal rings collapse, which causes a coughing or honking sound. Usually this coughing or honking is brought on by excitement over visiting a new dog or eating an especially tasty treat. As well, sometimes symptoms may be provoked by irritants in the environment, such as vehicle exhaust, smoke or dust.

Further, symptoms can be exacerbated when exercising during hot or humid weather, and more so if the dog is overweight. In mild cases, a honking or coughing session will only last for a few seconds and can be assisted by gently rubbing the dog's nose or giving a quick squeeze around the rib cage to help relax the trachea and get the air flowing again.

In severe cases, surgery is recommended, which involves applying prosthetic rings to the outside of the trachea. The success rate of this tricky operation is reported to be in the 75- to 85% range.

16) Undescended Testicles: occurs when a male dog's testicles are trapped in the abdominal cavity, which can sometimes be successfully treated with hormone injections. If the testicles still fail to descend they must be removed in order to prevent increased risk of becoming cancerous.

17) von Willebrand's Disease (vWD): is a blood disorder similar to hemophilia in humans. Poodles affected by the disease do not effectively utilize their platelets for blood clotting and therefore are more likely to have excessive bleeding episodes upon injury.

Fortunately, a simple DNA test is available so that you can find out at any time (without waiting for symptoms) whether your Miniature Poodle has inherited von Willebrand's disease.

Cocker Spaniel Health Concerns

A healthy Cocker Spaniel may or may not be plagued with health problems associated with their breed, and may live an average of 12 to 15 years or longer. Common genetic and other health problems that may afflict a Cocker Spaniel include:

1) Hip and Elbow Dysplasia: is a condition in which the head of the dog's femur does not fit correctly into the hip or elbow joint socket. Factors that have an influence include nutrition, as this is a dog that suffers from obesity, a dog's environment and the condition of the hips of its parents. Screening for hip dysplasia is recommended for breeding stock.

2) Luxating Patella: this slipping kneecap condition is a common defect seen in many breeds, including the Cocker Spaniel, that may also be caused by accidentally falling or jumping from a height. Often you will see a dog with this problem appear to be skipping down the road as they occasionally life one leg when the kneecap slips out of the patellar groove and the leg locks up.

Surgery is the treatment option for this condition, although many dogs live a relatively normal life with this defect.

3) Progressive Retinal Atrophy (PRA): some Cocker Spaniels can suffer from several eye problems, including Progressive Retinal Atrophy, which causes degeneration of the retina, which is the part of the eye that senses visual information and sends it to the brain.

Degeneration of this vital part of the eye eventually will lead to blindness. This disease usually appears between 3 and 5 years of age. A simple DNA test is available to determine (without waiting for symptoms to appear.

4) Cataracts: (which are common in many breeds), is an eye condition where the lens becomes cloudy or milky, which would be like trying to see through a foggy window. This eye condition can appear from birth to 3 years of age and will usually lead to blindness.

5) Glaucoma: this eye disease, which is usually caused by an increase of fluid pressure in the eye, can cause permanent damage to the dog's vision in the affected eye or eyes, which, if left untreated, can lead to blindness.

6) Ectropion: in a dog suffering from this condition the lower eyelid will turn outward and requires surgery to repair.

7) Entropion: is a condition in which the dog's eyelid will roll inward which then causes the lashes to rub against the eyeball. Left untreated, this condition can severely damage the dog's eye, even causing blindness. Surgery is required to correct this problem.

8) Cherry Eye: many breeds can suffer from this genetic eye problem, including the Cocker, where the gland of the third eyelid prolapses or slips in the corner of the eye, as a result of weakness of the connective tissue surrounding the gland, causing a pink fleshy protrusion to extend or bulge over the edge of the dog's eyelid.

Although it is possible for this problem to self-correct, it is recommended to take your dog to the veterinarian as soon as you notice this condition because treatment will require pushing the prolapsed gland back into the pocket.

9) Hemolytic Anemia: is a type of anemia caused by the abnormal breakdown of red blood cells in the blood vessels or other areas of the dog's body. This condition may be mild or life threatening.

10) Retinal Dysplasia: is an eye disease appears as streaks or dots in the retina of the dog's eye, which can lead to blindness.

11) Dilated Cardiomyopathy: this is a disease of the heart that causes that causes weakness in the muscle tissues and a subsequent enlarging of the heart.

12) Sick Sinus Syndrome: is another abnormality of the heart, where the heart beats irregularly causing an arrhythmia of the sinus node of the heart, which is the primary pacemaker of the heart. A dog suffering from this condition may experience low blood pressure.

13) Phosphofructokinase Deficiency: approximately 10% of the Cocker Spaniel population is affected by this condition, resulting from a recessive gene preventing the proper metabolizing of glucose into energy. A dog with this condition will be very low energy, preventing them from being able to exercise.

DNA testing is possible before breeding in order to prevent two dogs with the same recessive gene from producing puppies with this deficiency.

14) Epilepsy: approximately 10% of the Cocker Spaniel population can be genetically prone to canine epilepsy, which displays itself with mild to more serious seizures.

15) Rage Syndrome: this syndrome is also thought to be an inherited type of epilepsy, which appears as sudden, violent attacks in a dog that is otherwise calm and well behaved.

16) Ear Infections: because of their long hanging ears, these dogs are commonly prone to ear infection or inflammation, therefore, guardians need to make sure that the ears are kept dry after swimming or bathing and free of excessive hair.

2. Allergies

One of the most common complaints discussed at the veterinarian's office when they see dogs scratching and chewing at themselves is possible allergies.

Unlike us humans, who react to allergies with nasal symptoms, when our dogs are suffering from allergies they will typically present with itchy skin or ear problems.

a) Environmental: allergies are usually first noticed because your dog is scratching, itching, biting, licking or chewing at their skin or paws.

Just like us humans, our dogs can develop allergies to dust, chemicals, grass, mold, pollen, car exhaust, cigarette smoke, and flea and tick preparations, as well as allergies to materials such as wool or cotton, and chemicals found in washing soap or chemicals found in cleaning products you use around your home.

Symptoms are usually seen on the stomach, inside of the legs, and at the tail or paws.

Since most allergies are seasonal, our dogs will be more affected in the spring or fall. Airborne irritants inhaled by your Miniature Golden

Retriever, may result in coughing, sneezing or watery eyes.

If you think that your dog may have come in contact with an irritant found somewhere in your environment, the best thing to do for your dog is give them a cleansing bath, with the proper canine shampoo, followed by canine conditioner.

Remember that dogs are closer to the ground, and the longer and softer their coat, the more they resemble a duster who attracts everything they come into contact with.

b) Junk Food: *"True"* food allergies usually account for only about 10% of allergy problems in our canine friends.

For instance, itching, chewing and chronic ear infections are not actually caused by food allergies, but rather are the result of a suppressed immune system, which is caused by eating a low quality diet.

These types of food allergies can often be completely resolved by changing your Miniature Golden Retriever's diet to high quality food that is more easily digested. Proper nutrition is the easiest way to prevent any food allergies.

Many dog food products contain corn, wheat and soybeans, which are common allergens. Usually it is the gluten in these foods that cause the allergic reaction.
Visit your local pet food store and educate yourself or talk with a knowledgeable representative because there's no excuse for feeding your dog a junk food diet when there are so many healthy choices now available that will help your canine companion live a long and healthy life.

3. Canine CPR

Of course, nobody wants to ever be put in a situation where the life of their precious canine companion is put at risk, however, the reality is that accidents happen, and therefore knowing a little bit about how to help save your beloved furry friend is time well spent.

First of all, remember to handle an injured dog very carefully and gently. A dog that is traumatized, fearful or in pain, even one that is usually gentle, may lash out and try to bite.

Consider taking a class, because there are many animal CPR courses being offered these days through community educational systems or even online.

It's also a good idea to have a canine first aid kit both at home and in your vehicle in case of emergencies. Items to include in your first aid kit:

- Scissors
- Tweezers
- Tick Twister
- Nail Clippers
- Kwik Stop Styptic powder
- Gauze bandaging
- Non-stick bandages for wounds
- Medical tape
- Antiseptic wash for wounds (hydrogen peroxide)
- Sterile eyewash
- Towel
- Washcloth
- Blanket

Familiarizing yourself with the American Red Cross emergency techniques outlined in the following chart *("Saving your pet with CPR")* may be exactly what you need to help save the life of your own dog or someone else's.

Saving your pet with CPR

With pets increasingly being treated like a member of the family, many owners are learning emergency techniques like CPR to keep their pet alive before bringing it to a veterinarian.

If there is no breathing and no pulse, begin CPR immediately.

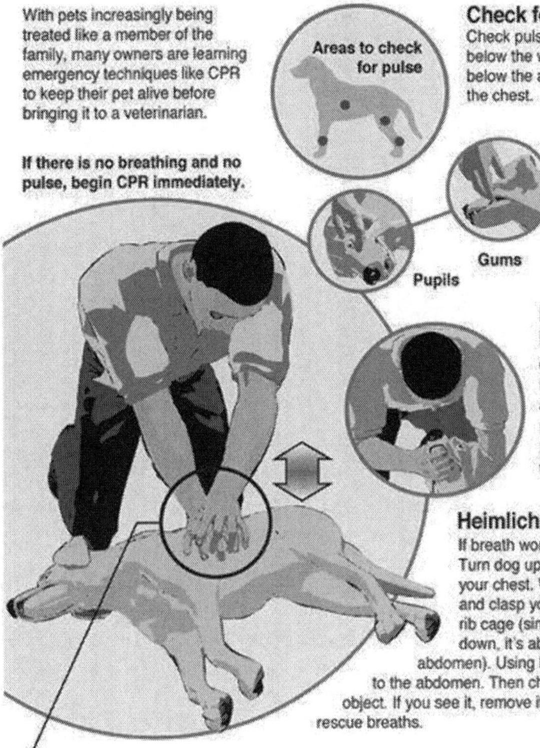

Check for breathing and pulse

Check pulse using middle and index finger below the wrist, inner thigh (femoral artery), below the ankle or where left elbow touches the chest.

Look for other warning signs

- Gums and lips will appear gray- colored.
- Pupils will be dilated and not responsive to light.

If not breathing, give breath to animal

Cats and small dogs
Place your mouth over its nose and mouth to blow air in.

Medium–large dogs
Place your mouth over its nose to blow air in.

Heimlich maneuver

If breath won't go in, airway may be blocked. Turn dog upside down, with its back against your chest. Wrap your arms around the dog and clasp your hands together just below its rib cage (since you're holding the dog upside down, it's above the rib cage, in the abdomen). Using both arms, give five sharp thrusts to the abdomen. Then check its mouth or airway for the object. If you see it, remove it and give two more rescue breaths.

Start compressions if no pulse

Lay animal on right side and place hand over ribs where its elbow touches the chest. Begin compressions. Do not give compressions if dog has pulse.

Animal size	Compress chest	Compressions per breath of air
Cat/small dog (Under 30 lbs.)	1/2-1 inch	5
Medium–large dog (30–90 lbs.)	1–3 inches	5
Giant dog (over 90 lbs.)	1–3 inches	10

Repeat procedure

- Check pulse after 1 minute and then every few minutes.
- Continue giving CPR until the animal has a pulse and is breathing.
- Stop CPR after 20 minutes.

SOURCE: American Red Cross

Chapter 9: Daily Feeding and Care

1. Feeding Puppies

For growing puppies, a general rule of thumb is to feed 10% of the puppy's present body weight or between 2% and 3% of their projected adult weight each day.

Keep in mind that high energy puppies will require extra protein to help them grow and develop into healthy adult dogs, especially during their first two years of life.

There are now many foods on the market that are formulated for all stages of a dog's life (including the puppy stage), so whether you choose one of these foods or a food specially formulated for puppies, they will need to be fed smaller meals more frequently throughout the day (3 or 4 times), until they are at least one year of age.

NOTE: choose quality sources of meat protein for healthy puppies and dogs, including beef, buffalo, chicken, duck, fish, hare, lamb, ostrich, pork, rabbit, turkey, venison, or any other source of wild meaty protein.

2. Feeding Adults

An adult dog will generally need to be fed between 2% and 3% of their body weight each day. Read the labels and avoid foods that contain a high amount of grains and other fillers. Choose foods that list high quality meat protein as the main ingredient.

Picky Eaters: be careful that you do not get into the habit of "doctoring" your dog's food with bits and pieces of your human food, otherwise you will inadvertently create a picky eater who will then refuse to eat.

If this has already happened and your dog is refusing to eat his or her dinner, so long as you are feeding a high quality (mostly meat) dog food, do not worry, because no dog will starve itself. In fact, if the dog were living in the wild, they would often go 2-3 days without catching any food. In order to break a dog of the habit of being a picky eater, make sure that you set regular meal times and remove food not eaten approximately 20

minutes after you have presented it to your dog.
It is important that your dog understands that you are in control of their food source, and once they understand this, they will also understand that they have a certain amount of time in which to eat their food.

It is also important to mix your dog's food with your hands, so that your scent is all over the food, before you give it to them to eat. This way you are mimicking what would happen if you were the pack leader out hunting for your food in the wild.

When dogs hunt for their own food, the leader of the pack always gets to eat first while all the other dogs must wait until the leader eats their fill before they can rush in to eat what is left over.

Therefore, when you are mixing your domesticated dog's dinner with your hands, and getting your scent all over the food, you are sending them the subtle message that you are the pack leader and that you are now allowing them to finish the food that was once yours.

TIP

GRATED Parmesan cheese sprinkled on a dog's dinner will help to stop picky eaters from ignoring their food while improving their skin and coat. To get the cheese to stick to the kibble, first mix a small amount of olive oil into the kibble, and then sprinkle with finely grated Parmesan cheese.

3. Treats

Since the creation of the first dog treat, over 150 years ago, the myriad of choices available in every pet store, feed store and grocery store shelf almost outnumbers those looking forward to eating them.

Today's treats are not just for making us feel better because it makes us happy to give our furry friends something they really enjoy; today's treats are also designed to actually improve our dog's health.

Some of us humans treat our dogs just because, others use treats for training purposes, others for health, while others treat for a combination of reasons.

Whatever reason you choose to give treats to your Miniature Golden Retriever, keep in mind that if we treat our dogs too often throughout the

day, we may create a picky eater who will no longer want to eat their regular meals.
As well, if the treats we are giving are high calorie, we may be putting our dog's health in jeopardy by allowing them to become overweight.

TIP

AN interesting article written by Jonathan O'Callaghan, recently published in June 12, 2014 in the Daily Mail, indicates that researchers in Sweden have discovered that dogs were visibly happier when they had to earn their treats as a reward for completing a task, rather than just being given a treat for looking cute.

Apparently, just like us humans get that happy "eureka" moment when we finally solve a problem, so do our canine counterparts.

If you've been treating your dog for no other reason that just because they looked expectantly at the cookie jar, perhaps now is the time to change your habits and ask your dog to perform a trick or to search for a hidden treat, so that your dog can also feel that emotional excitement of being rewarded for accomplishing a task.

4. Treats to Avoid

a) Rawhide: is soaked in an ash/lye solution to remove every particle of meat, fat and hair and then further soaked in bleach to remove remaining traces of the ash/lye solution. Now that the product is no longer food, it no longer has to comply with food regulations.

While the hide is still wet it is shaped into rawhide chews, and upon drying it shrinks to approximately 1/4 of its original size. Furthermore, arsenic based products are often used as preservatives, and antibiotics and insecticides are added to kill bacteria that also fight against good bacteria in your dog's intestines.

The collagen fibres in the rawhide make it very tough and long lasting, which makes this chew a popular choice for humans to give to their dogs because it satisfies the dog's natural urge to chew while providing many hours of quiet entertainment.

Sadly, when a dog chews a rawhide treat, they ingest many harsh chemicals and when your dog swallows a piece of rawhide, that piece can swell up to four times its size inside your dog's stomach, which can cause anything from mild to severe gastric blockages that could become life threatening and require surgery.

b) Pig's Ears: are actually the ears of pigs, and while most dogs will eagerly devour them, they are extremely high in fat, which can cause stomach upsets, vomiting and diarrhea for many dogs. Pig's ears are often processed and preserved with unhealthy chemicals that discerning dog guardians will not want to feed their dogs.

The pig ears are quite thin and crispy and when the dog chews them pieces can break off, like chips, and can easily become stuck in a dog's throat. While pig's ears are generally not considered to be a healthy treat choice for any dog, they should be especially avoided for any dog that may be at risk of being overweight.

c) Hoof Treats: many humans give cow, horse and pig hooves to their dogs as treats because they consider them to be *"natural"* when the truth is that after processing these *"treats"* they retain little, if any, of their *"natural"* qualities.

Hoof treats are processed with harsh preservatives, including insecticides, lead, bleach, arsenic based products, and antibiotics to kill bacteria that can also harm the good bacteria in your dog's intestines, and if all bacteria is not killed in these meat-based products before feeding them to your dog, they could also suffer from Salmonella poisoning.

Hooves are very hard and can also cause the chipping or breaking of your dog's teeth as well as perforation or blockages in your dog's intestines.

5. Healthy Treats

Yes, we love to treat our dogs, whether for helping to teach the new puppy to go pee outside, teaching the adolescent dog new commands, for trick training, for general good behavior, or for no reason at all, other than that they just gave us the *"look"*.

a) Hard Treats: there are so many choices of hard or crunchy treats available that come in many varieties of shapes, sizes and flavors that you may have a difficult time choosing. If your dog will eat them, hard treats will help to keep their teeth cleaner.

Whatever you do choose, be certain to read the labels and make sure that the ingredients are high quality and appropriately sized for your Miniature

Golden Retriever friend.
b) Soft Treats: are also available in endless varieties and flavors, suitable for all the different needs of our furry friends and are often used for training purposes as they have a stronger smell.
c) Dental Treats or Chews: are designed with the specific purpose of helping your dog to maintain healthy teeth and gums. They usually require intensive chewing and are often shaped with high ridges and bumps to exercise the jaw and massage gums while removing plaque build-up near the gum line.

d) Freeze-Dried and Jerky Treats: offer a tasty morsel most dogs find irresistible as they are usually made of simple, meaty ingredients, such as liver, poultry and seafood. These treats are usually lightweight and easy to carry around, which means they can also be great as training treats.

e) Human Food Treats: you will want to be very careful when feeding human foods to dogs as treats, because many of our foods contain additives and ingredients that could be toxic and harmful.

Be certain to choose simple, fresh foods with minimal or no processing, such as lean meat, poultry or seafood, and even if your dog will eat anything put in front of them, be aware that many common human foods such as grapes, raisins, onions and chocolate are poisonous to dogs.

f) Training Treats: while any sort of treat can be used as an extra incentive during training sessions, soft treats are often used for training purposes because of their stronger smell and smaller sizes.

Generally, the treats you feed your dog should not make up more than approximately 10% of their daily food intake, so make sure the treats you choose are high quality, so that you can help to keep your Miniature Golden Retriever both happy and healthy.

6. Choosing the Right Food

In order to choose the right food for your Miniature Golden Retriever, first it's important to understand a little bit about canine physiology and what Mother Nature intended when she created our fur friends.

More than 230 years ago, in 1785, the English Sportman's dictionary described the best diet for a dog's health in an article entitled *"Dog"*. This article indicated that the best food for a dog was something called

"Greaves", described as "the sediment of melted tallow. It is made into cakes for dogs' food. In Scotland and parts of the US it is called cracklings."

Out of the meager beginning of the first commercially made dog food has sprung a massively lucrative and vastly confusing industry that has only recently begun to evolve beyond those early days of feeding our dogs the dregs of human leftovers because it was cheap and convenient for us.

Even today, the majority of dog food choices have far more to do with being convenient for humans to store and serve than it does with being a diet truly designed to be a nutritionally balanced, healthy food choice for a canine.

The dog food industry is big business and as such, because there are now almost limitless choices, there is much confusion and endless debate when it comes to answering the question, *"What is the best food for my dog?"*

Educating yourself by talking to experts and reading everything you can find on the subject, plus taking into consideration several relevant factors, will help to answer the dog food question for you and your dog.

For instance, where you live may dictate what sorts of foods you have access to. Other factors to consider will include the particular requirements of your dog, such as their age, energy and activity levels.

Next will be expense, time and quality. While we all want to give our dogs the best food possible, many humans lead very busy lives and cannot, for instance, prepare their own dog food, but still want to feed a high quality diet that fits within their budget.

However, perhaps most important when choosing an appropriate diet for our dogs is learning to be more observant of Mother Nature's design and taking a closer look at our dog's teeth, jaws and digestive tract in order to truly understand what is best for our dogs.

While humans are herbivores who derive energy from eating plants, our canine companions are carnivores, which means that they derive their energy and nutrient requirements from eating a diet consisting mainly or exclusively of the flesh of animal tissues (in other words, meat).

a) The Canine Teeth: the first part of your dog you will want to take a good look at when considering what to feed will be their teeth. Unlike humans, who are equipped with wide, flat molars for grinding grains, vegetables and other plant-based materials, canine teeth are all pointed because they are designed to rip, shred and tear into animal meat and bone.

b) The Canine Jaw: is another obvious consideration when choosing an appropriate food source is the fact that every canine is born equipped with powerful jaws and neck muscles for the specific purpose of being able to pull down and tear apart their hunted prey.

The structure of the jaw of every canine is such that it opens widely to hold large pieces of meat and bone, while the actual mechanics of a dog's jaw permits only vertical (up and down) movement that is designed for crushing.

c) The Canine Digestive Tract: a dog's digestive tract is short and simple and designed to move their natural choice of food (hide, meat and bone) quickly through their systems.

Vegetables and plant matter require more time to break down in the gastrointestinal tract, which in turn, requires a more complex digestive system than the canine body is equipped with.

The canine digestive system is simply unable to break down vegetable matter, which is why whole vegetables look pretty much the same going into your dog as they do coming out the other end.

Given the choice, most dogs would never choose to eat plants or vegetables and fruits over meat, however, we continue to feed them a kibble-based diet that contains high amounts of vegetables, fruits and grains and low amounts of meat.

Plus, in order to get our dogs to eat fruits, vegetables and grains we usually have to flavor the food with meat or meat by-products.

How much healthier and long-lived might our beloved friends be if, instead of largely ignoring nature's design for our canine companions, we chose to feed them whole, unprocessed, species-appropriate food?

With many hundreds of dog food brands to choose from, it's no wonder we humans are confused about what to feed our dogs to help them live long and healthy lives. The following are some suggestions and questions that may help you choose a dog food company that you can feel comfortable with:

- How long have they have been in business?
- Is dog food their main industry?
- Are they dedicated to their brand?
- Are they easily accessible?
- Do they honestly answer your questions?
- Do they have a good Company Safety Standard?
- Do they set higher standards?
- Read the ingredients - where did they come from?
- Are the ingredients something you would eat?
- Are the ingredients farmed locally?
- Was it cooked using standards you would trust?
- Is the company certified under human food or organic guidelines?

Whatever you decide to feed your Miniature Golden Retriever, keep in mind that, just as too much wheat, other grains and other fillers in our human diet is having detrimental effects on our health, the same can be very true for our pets.

Our dogs are also suffering from many of the same life threatening diseases that are commonly found in our human society (heart disease, cancer, diabetes, obesity), which all have a direct correlation with eating genetically altered foods that are no longer pure, in favor of a convenient, processed and packaged diet.

7. The Raw Diet

While more and more of us humans are coming to the belief that we are killing ourselves and our dogs with processed foods, others believe that there are dangers involved in feeding raw foods to our fur friends.

Those who are raw feeding advocates believe that the ideal diet for their dog is one which would be very similar to what a dog living in the wild would have access to hunting or foraging, and these canine guardians are often opposed to feeding their dog any sort of commercially manufactured pet foods, because they consider them to be poor substitutes.

On the other hand, those opposed to feeding their dogs a raw or biologically appropriate raw food diet believe that the risks associated with food-borne illnesses, during the handling and feeding of raw meats,

outweigh the purported benefits.
Interestingly, even though the United States Food and Drug Administration (FDA) states that they do not advocate a raw diet for dogs, they do advise those who wish to take this route, that following basic hygiene guidelines for handling raw meat can minimize any associated risks.

Furthermore, high pressure pasteurization (HPP), which is high pressure, water-based technology for killing bacteria, is USDA-approved for use on organic and natural food products, and is being utilized by many commercial raw pet food manufacturers.

Raw meats purchased at your local grocery store contain a much higher level of acceptable bacteria than raw food produced for dogs because the meat purchased for human consumption is supposed to be cooked, which will kill any bacteria that might be present. This means that canine guardians feeding their dogs a raw food diet can be quite certain that commercially prepared raw foods sold in pet stores will be safer than raw meats purchased in grocery stores.

Many guardians of high energy, working breed dogs will agree that their dogs thrive on a raw or BARF (Biologically Appropriate Raw Food) diet and strongly believe that the potential benefits of feeding a raw dog food diet are many, including:

- Healthy, shiny coats
- Decreased shedding
- Fewer allergy problems
- Healthier skin
- Cleaner teeth
- Fresher breath
- Increased energy levels
- Improved digestion
- Smaller stools
- Strengthened immune system
- Increased mobility in arthritic pets
- Increase or improvement in overall health

All dogs of every size, whether working breed or companion dogs, are amazing athletes in their own right, therefore every dog deserves to be fed the best food available.

A raw diet is a direct evolution of what dogs ate before they became our domesticated pets and we turned toward commercially prepared, easy to serve dry dog food that required no special storage or preparation. The BARF diet is all about feeding our dogs what they are designed to eat by returning them to their wild, evolutionary diet.

8. The Dehydrated Diet

Dehydrated dog food comes in both raw meat and cooked meat forms and these foods are usually air dried to reduce moisture to the level where bacterial growth is inhibited.

The appearance of de-hydrated dog food is very similar to dry kibble and the typical feeding methods include adding warm water before serving, which makes this type of diet both healthy for our dogs and convenient for us to serve.

Dehydrated recipes are made from minimally processed fresh whole foods to create a healthy and nutritionally balanced meal that will meet or exceed the dietary requirements of a healthy canine. Dehydrating removes only the moisture from the fresh ingredients, which usually means that because the food has not already been cooked at a high temperature, more of the overall nutrition is retained.

A dehydrated diet is a convenient way to feed your dog a nutritious diet because all you have to do is add warm water and wait five minutes while the food re-hydrates so your Miniature Golden Retriever can enjoy a warm meal.

9. The Kibble Diet

While many canine guardians are starting to take a closer look at the food choices they are making for their furry companions, there is no mistaking that the convenience and relative economy of dry dog food kibble, which had its beginnings in the 1940‘s, continues to be the most popular pet food choice for many dog-friendly humans.

Some 75 years later, the massive pet food industry offers up a confusingly large number of choices with hundreds of different manufacturers and brand names lining the shelves of veterinarian offices, grocery stores and pet food aisles.

NOTE: as a general rule of thumb, the best pet foods are NOT found in the grocery isle of your local supermarket. Take the time to buy your food

from a pet store.
While feeding a high quality bagged kibble diet that has been flavored to appeal to dogs and supplemented with vegetables and fruits to appeal to humans may keep most canine companions happy and relatively healthy, you will ultimately need to decide whether this is the best diet for them.

10. The Right Bowl

Here is a brief description of the different categories and types of dog bowls that would be appropriate choices for your dog's particular needs.

Keeping in mind that the Miniature Golden Retriever may be highly food motivated, it may be a good idea to get them a slow feeder type of bowl to slow down the speed at which they consume their food.

Automatic Watering Bowls: are standard dog bowls (often made out of plastic) that are attached to a reservoir container, which is designed to keep water constantly available to your dog as long as there is water remaining in the storage compartment.

Ceramic/Stoneware Bowls: an excellent choice for those who like options in personality, color and shape.

Elevated Bowls: raised dining table dog bowls are a tidy and classy choice that will make your dog's dinner time a more comfortable experience while getting the bowls off the floor.

No Skid Bowls: are for dogs that push their bowls across the floor when eating. A non-skid dog bowl will help keep the food bowl where you put it.

No Tip Bowls: are designed to prevent the messy type of doggy eater from flipping over their dinner or water bowls.

Slow Feeder Bowls: many of our canine companions eat their food so quickly that it can literally cause health issues, such as choking, digestion problems, throwing up, and bloating that can cause death from gulping too much air with their food.

These special bowls are known by several different names, including *"Anti-Gulp", "Go Slow", "Slow Feeder"*, and *"Slow Me Down"*, and if your dog is wolfing their food, this will be the best type of bowl for them.

If you don't want to spend the money on a specialty slow feeder bowl, find yourself a fist-sized, smooth round rock and place it in the middle of your dog's stainless bowl so they have to work their way around the rock to get to their food. This will do the job of slowing them down just as effectively.

Stainless Steel Bowls: are as close to indestructible as a bowl can be, plus they are sanitary, easy to clean and water stays cooler for a longer period of time in a stainless bowl.

Wooden Bowls: for those humans concerned about stylish home decor, wooden dog bowl dining stations are beautiful pieces of furniture unto themselves that can enhance your home decor.

Travel Bowls: are convenient, practical and handy additions for every canine travel kit.

Consider a space saving, collapsible dog bowl, made out of hygienic, renewable bamboo that comes in fun colors and different sizes, making it perfect for every travel bowl need.

If you would like to learn more about all the many dog bowl choices available, visit DogBowlForYourDog.com, which is a comprehensive, one-stop website dedicated to explaining the ins and outs of every food bowl imaginable and helping you find the perfect bowl for all your Miniature Golden Retriever's needs.

11. Exercise

All of our canine companions are amazing, natural athletes and because of this, they need daily exercise to stay fit, happy and healthy. The highly energetic Miniature Golden Retriever is no exception to this rule.

Every Miniature Golden Retriever has a great deal of stamina and will require plenty of daily exercise. They will love going for walks or engaging in any manner of canine sport with their guardian several times every day as well as playing in a pack of other dogs.

In addition, taking your Miniature Golden Retriever for a disciplined walk, where they are on a leash and calmly walking beside you without straining on the leash or trying to lead you, will reinforce that you are the boss and they are the follower.

Any type of disciplined exercise you can engage in with your dog will help to exercise both their body and their intelligent mind and will burn off pent-up daily energy reserves so that your Miniature Golden Retriever will be a happy and contented companion.

If you find that your Miniature Golden Retriever is being a pest by chewing inappropriate items around the home or being demanding of your time, or especially unruly when visitors come to call, this is likely because they are not being challenged enough or exercised often enough, or long enough each day to drain out their daily pent-up energy reserves.

A healthy, adult Miniature Golden Retriever will thrive when being walked several times each day and may also enjoy the challenge of being engaged in other forms of disciplined activity.

12. Playtime

Every dog needs some regular playtime each day, and while every Miniature Golden Retriever will be different with respect to what types of games they may enjoy, most will really love any game involving retrieving food.

A fun game of *"Search"*, where you ask your dog to "Sit/Stay" while you hide a favorite treat that they then have to use their nose to find, will appeal to almost every Miniature Golden Retriever.

After a disciplined walk with your dog, they will also enjoy being given the opportunity for some off leash freedom to really stretch out by running free to play and socialize with other similar sized dogs.

13. Daily Grooming

Daily grooming is a must for any healthy dog, so make sure that you get into the routine of spending at least 15 minutes each day brushing or combing your dog, checking their ears and nails and brushing their teeth.

14. Safe Traveling

Far too many canine guardians do nothing to protect their companions when traveling with them inside their vehicles.
According to a 2011 American Automobile Association study, only about

16% of dog owners restrain their pets when riding in a vehicle, and of those who are trying, many are not properly securing their beloved pets.

That leaves 84% of people who let their dogs roam freely about the inside of their vehicles, leaving them at serious risk of being injured or killed in an automobile accident.
For example, when a vehicle traveling at only 30 miles per hour (48.28 kilometers per hour) is involved in an accident, a small, ten pound (4.54 kg), unrestrained dog will be subjected to approximately 300 pounds force (136 kilogram-force), which is certainly enough to seriously injure or snap the neck of a Miniature Golden Retriever.

There is no denying that dogs that are not properly restrained become projectiles in any sort of vehicle crash.

Many drivers permit their smaller dogs to sit on their lap when driving, which is not only distracting to the driver, but if involved in an accident, the dog can be seriously injured or killed if they are thrown threw a window.

a) Faulty Restraints: many dog lovers may be laboring under the misconception that they are doing the right thing by buckling their canine companions into a safety harness because they are unaware that many of these dog harnesses that are supposed to keep furry passengers safe have a 100% failure rate.

Statistics collected by the Center for Pet Safety (CPS) have shown that every popular restraint tested with dog dummies, traveling at a sedate 30 mph (48.28 km/h), not only failed, but also indicated that serious injuries or deaths were highly likely.

Most restraints that were tested in the CPS study allowed dogs to easily become flying projectiles during vehicle accidents because the harnesses were simply not strong enough to keep them in their seats, and in many cases the restraints could actually choke the dog during a crash.

When the MGA Research Corporation carried out a pilot study for The Center for Pet Safety (CPS), in which they tested 12 major brands of pet harnesses, the results indicated a **100% failure rate**.

According to the American Kennel Club, these safety harness tests were carried out using the average weights of the ten most popular breeds of dogs.

The founder and chairman of CPS believes, "Saying that these products prevent your pet from becoming a projectile in an accident is a potentially misleading statement."

Law enforcement agencies, safety advocates, insurance companies, and concerned dog owners need to keep pressing for the development of a standard for dog safety equipment, to insist that all such equipment pass a government regulated crash test before being sold as safe for travel.

The safest travel arrangement for any dog is to secure them inside a kennel, followed by finding a safety restraint that is crash and strength tested and certified to be safe for your dog.

b) Kennels: if you opt to contain your best friend inside a kennel or crate, you absolutely must make sure that the kennel is very securely attached with the vehicle's seatbelt system or even better, with special tie downs that are bolted to the floor of the vehicle.

A dog kennel or crate will easily fit (sideways) on the back seat of most vehicles and can be secured with the vehicle's restraint system and a dog riding inside a kennel that is secure inside your vehicle will have the best protection in the case of a rollover accident.

As well, for maximum safety and security when travelling with your dog, you might wish to go the extra mile and spend the extra dollars to buy them a "Mim VarioCage".

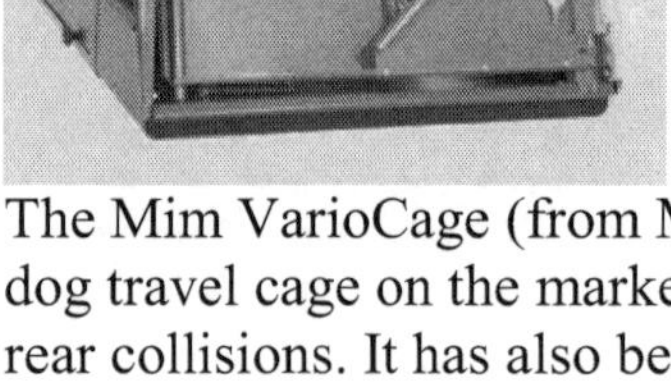

The Mim VarioCage (from Mighty Mite Dog Gear) is apparently the only dog travel cage on the market today that has been tested in both frontal and rear collisions. It has also been in a drop test, which simulates a rollover with a car, and crash tests have been carried out by the Technical Research Institute of Sweden. This kennel is designed to fit into the cargo carrying area of a vehicle.

c) Harness Restraints: the Kurgo Tru-Fit Smart harness has been crash and strength tested and with its steel nesting buckles has a tensile strength tested to withstand a force of 2250 pounds (1020 kilogram-force). The crash test videos of this product depict a 35-pound (15.9 kilogram) dummy dog traveling at 30 miles per hour (48.28 km/h), recorded at an accredited University test facility.

The Ruff Rider Roadie® harness successfully passed the preliminary test criteria for both dynamic and static load limits. Ruff Rider's only product is the Roadie® travel restraint, which was invented by dog owner Carl Goldberg after his pet was ejected through the front windshield of his vehicle during a minor collision.

The design of the Roadie® is so unique that it was awarded three patents, and over the past 20 years Roadie® has helped protect many dogs during vehicle accidents.

Sleepypod™ manufactures a safety harness called *"Clickit Utility"* that has a #1 safety rating. Apparently, this harness is the first dog safety harness to incorporate three-points of attachment to better absorb force caused in a front end collision by effectively dissipating energy while keeping the dog in the car seat during an impact (patents pending).

The Clickit Utility harness can also be used in the cargo area and includes a d-ring on the back of the vest so it can be used as a walking harness.

Keep your Miniature Golden Retriever safe when traveling in your vehicle. Do your research and either transport your dog inside a kennel, or find a safety harness that is both strength tested and certified to be able to keep your dog safe in the event of an accident.

d) Air Travel: the Miniature Golden Retriever will be too large to travel comfortably inside a Sherpa bag inside the airplane cabin when they are full grown, and can be *"carry on baggage"* as puppies if the carrier conforms to the airline regulations, which state that a pet carrier must be able to fit under the seat in front of you.

Most soft carriers are airline approved and under seat dimensions are generally as follows:
Window Seat: 19" L x 14" W x 8.25" H

[48.26 cm L x 35.56 cm W x 20.955 cm H]
Middle Seat: 19" L x 19" W x 8.25" H
[48.26 cm L x 48.26 cm W x 20.955 cm H]
Aisle Seat: 19" L x 14" W x 8.25" H
[48.26 cm L x 35.56 cm W x 20.955 cm H]

For in-cabin travel by plane, your puppy must be able to stand up and turn around comfortably inside the bag. Airlines also require an absorbent liner in the bag, which could be a pee pad, an old towel, a favorite blanket, or a cozy, faux lambskin liner.

Many styles of canine carrier bags are officially approved for airline travel, and when you make your flight reservations, don't forget to reserve for your Miniature Golden Retriever puppy as well because there is generally a small charge for in-cabin travel and some airlines will only permit a certain number of canine travelers per flight.

Any puppy or dog that is too large to fit inside a Sherpa bag will need to be transported inside a securely fastened, hard-sided kennel inside the airplane cargo hold.

Chapter 10: House Training

1. Human Training

House training, house breaking, or *"potty"* training is a critical first step in the education of any new puppy, and the first part of a successful process is training the human guardian. When you bring home your new puppy, they will be relying on your guidance to teach them what they need to learn.

When you provide your puppy with your consistent patience and understanding, they are capable of learning rules at a very early age, and house training is no different, especially since it's all about establishing a regular routine.

Potty training a new puppy takes time and patience — how much time depends entirely upon you.

Make sure your energy remains consistently calm and patient and that you exercise plenty of compassion and understanding while you help your new puppy learn their new bathroom rules.

All puppies and dogs flourish with routines and happily so do humans, therefore the first step will be to establish a daily routine that will work well for both canine and human alike.

For instance, depending upon the age of your puppy, make a plan to take them out for a bathroom break every two hours and stick to it because while you are in the beginning stages of potty training, the more vigilant and consistent you can be, the quicker and more successful your results will be.

Generally speaking, while your puppy is still growing, a young puppy can hold it approximately one hour for every month of their age. This means that if your 2-month-old puppy has been happily snoozing for a couple of hours, as soon as they wake up, they will need to go outside.

Some of the first indications or signs that your puppy needs to be taken outside to relieve themselves will be when you see them:
Some of the first indications or signs that your puppy needs to be taken outside to relieve themselves will be when you see them:

- Sniffing around
- Circling
- Looking for or approaching the door
- Whining, crying or barking
- Scratching at the door
- Acting agitated

It will be important to always take your puppy out first thing every morning, and immediately after they wake up from a nap as well as soon after they have finished eating a meal or having a big drink of water. Also, your happy praise goes a long way toward encouraging and reinforcing future success when your puppy makes the right decisions, so let them know you are happy when they do their business in the right place.

Initially, treats can be a good way to reinforce how pleased you are that your puppy is learning to go potty in the right place. Slowly treats can be removed and replaced with your happy praise.

Next, now that you have a new puppy in your life, you will want to be flexible with respect to adapting your schedule to meet the requirements that will help to quickly teach your puppy their new bathroom routine.

This means not leaving your puppy alone for endless hours at a time because firstly, they are sensitive pack animals that need companionship and your direction at all times, plus long periods alone will result in the disruption of the potty training schedule you have worked hard to establish.

If you have no choice but to leave your puppy alone for many hours, make sure that you place them in a paper lined room or pen where they can relieve themselves without destroying your favorite carpet or new hardwood flooring.

Remember, your Miniature Golden Retriever is a growing puppy with a bladder and bowels that they do not yet have complete control over and you will have a much happier time and better success if you simply train yourself to pay attention to when your young companion is showing signs of needing to relieve themselves.

2. Bell Training

A very easy way to introduce your new puppy to house training is to begin by teaching them how to ring a doorbell whenever they need to go outside.

Ringing a doorbell is not only a convenient alert system for both you and your puppy or dog, your visitors will be most impressed by how smart your Miniature Golden Retriever is.

A further benefit of training your puppy to ring a bell is that you will not have to listen to your puppy or dog whining, barking or howling to be let out, and your door will not become scratched up from their nails.

Unless you prefer to purchase an already manufactured doggy doorbell or system, take a trip to your local novelty store and purchase a small bell that has a nice, loud ring.

Attach the bell to a piece of ribbon or string and hang it from a door handle or tape it to a doorsill near the door where you will be taking your puppy out when they need to relieve themselves. The string will need to be long enough so that your puppy can easily reach the bell with their nose or a paw.

Next, each time you take your puppy out to go potty, say the word *"Out"*, and use their paw or their nose to ring the bell. Praise them for this *"trick"* and immediately take them outside.

The only down side to teaching your puppy or dog to ring a bell when they want to go outside is that even if they don't actually have to go out to relieve themselves, but just want to go outside because they are bored, you will still have to take them out every time they ring the bell.

There are many types and styles of *"gotta' go"* commercially manufactured bells you could choose, ranging from the elegant **"Poochie Bells™"** that hang from a doorknob, the simple **"Tell Bell™"** that sits on the floor, or various high tech door chime systems that function much like a doggy intercom system where they push a pad with their paw and it rings a bell. Whatever doorbell system you choose for your puppy, once they are trained, this type of an alert system is an easy way to eliminate accidents in the home.

3. Kennel Training

Kennel training is always a good idea for any puppy early in their education, because it can be utilized for many different situations, including keeping them safe while traveling inside a vehicle and being a very helpful tool for house training.

When purchasing a kennel for your puppy, always buy a kennel that will be the correct size for your puppy once they become an adult.

The kennel will be the correct size if an adult Miniature Golden Retriever can stand up and easily turn around inside their kennel.

When you train your puppy to accept sleeping in their own kennel at nighttime, this will also help to accelerate their potty training, because no puppy or dog wants to relieve themselves where they sleep, which means that they will hold their bladder and bowels as long as they possibly can.

Always be kind and compassionate and remember that a puppy will be able to hold it approximately one hour for every month of their age.

Generally, a puppy that is three months old will be able to hold it for approximately three hours, unless they just ate a meal or had a big drink of water.

Be watchful and consistent so that you learn your puppy's body language, which will alert you to when it's time for them to go outside.

Presenting them with familiar scents, by taking them to the same spot in the yard or the same street corner, will help to remind and encourage them that they are outside to relieve themselves.

Use a voice cue to remind your puppy why they are outside, such as *"go pee"* and always remember to praise them every time they relieve themselves in the right place so that they quickly understand what you expect of them and will learn to *"go"* on cue.

4. Exercise Pen Training

The exercise pen is a transition from kennel only training and will be helpful for those times when you may have to leave your puppy for more hours than they can reasonably be expected to hold it.

During those times when you must be away from the home for several hours, it's time to introduce your puppy to an exercise pen.

Exercise pens are usually constructed of wire sections that you can put together in whatever shape you desire, and the pen needs to be large enough to hold your puppy's kennel inside one half of the pen, while the

other half will be lined with newspapers or pee pads.
Place your puppy's food and water dishes next to the kennel and leave the kennel door open, so they can wander in and out whenever they wish, to eat or drink or go to the papers or pads if they need to relieve themselves.

Your puppy will be contained in a small area of your home while you are away and because they are already used to sleeping inside their kennel, they will not want to relieve themselves inside the area where they sleep. Therefore, your puppy will naturally go to the other half of the pen to relieve themselves on the newspapers or pee pads.

This method will help train your puppy to be quickly "paper" trained when you must leave them alone for a few hours.

5. Puppy Apartment™ Training

A similar and more costly alternative, the *Puppy Apartment*™ is a step up from the exercise pen training system that makes the process of crate or pen training even easier on both humans and puppies.

The Puppy Apartment™ works well in a variety of situations, whether you're at home and unable to pay close attention to your puppy's needs, whether you must be away from the home for a few hours or during the evening when everyone is asleep and you don't particularly want to get up at 3:00 a.m. to take your puppy out to go pee.

The Puppy Apartment™ is an innovation that is convenient for both puppy and human alike. What makes this system so effective is the patent pending dividing wall with a door leading to the other side, all inside the pen.

One side of the Puppy Apartment™ is where the puppy's bed is located and the other side (through the doorway) is the bathroom area that is lined with pee pads. With the bathroom right next door, your puppy or dog can take a bathroom break whenever they wish, without the need to alert family members to let them out.

This one bedroom, one bathroom system, which is a combination of the kennel/training pen, is a great alternative for helping to eliminate the stress of worrying about always keeping a watchful eye on your puppy or getting up during the night to take them outside every few hours to help them avoid making mistakes.

According to Modern Puppies...

> *"The Puppy Apartment™ takes the MESSY out of paper training, the ODORS AND HASSLES out of artificial grass training, MISSING THE MARK out of potty pad training and HAVING TO HOLD IT out of crate training. House training a puppy has never been faster or easier!*
>
> *The Puppy Apartment™ has taken all the benefits of the most popular potty training methods and combined them into one magical device and potty training system. This device and system has revolutionized how modern puppies are potty trained!"*

Manufactured in the United States, this product ships directly from the California supplier (Modern Puppies). Pricing of the Puppy Apartment™ begins at $138. USD (£83.37) and is only available online at Modern Puppies.

6. Free Training

If you would rather not confine your young puppy to one or two rooms in your home, and will be allowing them to freely range about your home anywhere they wish during the day, this is considered free training.

When free house training your Miniature Golden Retriever puppy, you will need to closely watch your puppy's activities all day long so that you can be aware of the *"signs"* that will indicate when they need to go outside to relieve themselves. For instance, circling and sniffing is a sure sign that they are looking for a place to do their business.

Never get upset or scold a puppy for having an accident inside the home, because this will result in teaching your puppy to be afraid of you and to only relieve themselves in secret places or when you're not watching.

If you catch your puppy making a mistake, all that is necessary is for you to calmly say *"No"*, and quickly scoop them up and take them outside or to their indoor bathroom area.

From your sensitive puppy's point of view, yelling or screaming when they make a potty mistake will be understood by your puppy or dog as unstable energy being displayed by the person who is supposed to be their leader. This type of unstable behavior will only teach your puppy to fear and disrespect you.

When you are vigilant, most puppies are not difficult to housebreak and they will generally do very well when you start them off with *"puppy pee pads"* that you will move closer and closer to the same door that you always use when taking them outside. This way they will quickly learn to associate going to this door when they need to relieve themselves.

When you pay close attention to your puppy's sleeping, eating, drinking and playing habits, you will quickly learn their body language so that you are able to predict when they might need to relieve themselves.

Your puppy will always need to relieve themselves first thing in the morning, as soon as they wake up from a nap, approximately 20 minutes after they finish eating a meal, after they have finished a play session, and of course, before they go to bed at night.

It's important to have compassion during this house training time in your young dog's life so that their education will be as stress-free as possible.

It's also important to be vigilant because how well you pay attention will minimize the opportunities your puppy may have for making a bathroom mistake in the first place, and the fewer mistakes they make, the sooner your puppy will be house trained.

7. Mistakes Happen

Remember that a dog's sense of smell is at least 2,000 times more sensitive that our human sense of smell.

As a result, it will be very important to effectively remove all odors from house training accidents, because otherwise your puppy will be attracted by the smell to the place where they may have had a previous accident, and will want to do their business there again and again.

While there are many products that are supposed to remove odors and stains, many of these are not very effective. You want a professional grade cleaner that will not just mask one odor with another scent – you want a product that will completely neutralize odors.

TIP

GO TO RemoveUrineOdors.com and order yourself some *"SUN"* and/or

"Max Enzyme" because these products contain professional-strength odor neutralizers and urine digesters that bind to and completely absorb odors on any type of surface.

8. Electronic Training Devices

Generally speaking, positive training methods are far more effective than using devices that involve negative stimulation.

Furthermore, unless you are training a Miniature Golden Retriever to hunt badgers or rabbits, using electronic devices is usually an excuse for a lazy human who will not take the time to properly train their dog by teaching them rules and boundaries, which leads to respect and an attentive follower.

When you do not provide your Miniature Golden Retriever (or any dog) with a consistent leadership role that teaches your dog to trust, respect and listen to you in all circumstances, you will inevitably experience behavioral issues.

Electronic training devices such as e-collars, spray collars or electronic fencing all rely upon negative, painful or stressful reinforcement, which can easily cause a puppy or dog to become nervous or live a life of fear.

For instance, a dog simply cannot understand the principles of "invisible" boundaries, and therefore should never be subjected to the confusion of the punishment that occurs when walking across an invisible line within their own home territory.

Dogs naturally understand the positive training methods of receiving a reward, which is not only much more efficient and effective when teaching boundaries, rewards are far kinder, and create a much stronger bond with your dog.

a) The Truth About Shock Collars: first of all, it would have to be an extremely rare situation in which it would be necessary or recommended that you use a shock collar on a Miniature Golden as these devices are usually only employed in extreme situations, and generally for much larger breeds whose aggressive behavior could seriously harm someone.

The use of remote, electronic, shock or *"e-collars"* is at best a controversial subject that can quickly escalate into heated arguments.

In certain, rare circumstances, and when used correctly, the e-collar can be a helpful training tool that could actually save a dog's life if they are acting out in dangerous ways that could seriously harm or even kill them (i.e. chasing vehicles).

An e-collar would generally be utilized in a circumstance where a larger breed of dog has access to free range over a large property, resulting in difficulties getting their attention from a distance if they become distracted by other animals or smells.

Many dogs that have not been properly trained from a young age also learn that when they are off leash and out of your immediate reach they can choose to ignore your commands, bark their heads off, terrorize the neighbors or chase wildlife.

All of these situations are generally not activities that a Miniature Golden Retriever would have the slightest interest in, unless they have access to a large property and their hunting instinct kicks in, because they would prefer being at home with their humans.

Generally, e-collars can be effective training tools for working breed herding, hunting or tracking dogs and in these types of circumstances a remote training collar can be an effective training device for reinforcing verbal commands from a great distance, such as "Come", "Sit" or "Stay".

Finally, electronic collars can be used as a last resort to help teach a dog not to engage in a dangerous behavior that could result in them being seriously harmed or even killed.

b) Electronic Fencing: honestly, there are far more reasons NOT to install an electronic fence as a means of keeping your dog inside your yard than there are good reasons for considering one.

In most cases, people who install electronic fencing because they are worried that their dog will run away have simply not taken the time to develop a relationship of trust and respect with their canine companion.

For instance, a dog whose yard is surrounded by an electronic fence can quite easily develop fear, aggression, or both, directed toward what they may believe is the cause of the shock they are receiving.

As a result, installing an electronic fence may cause your Miniature Golden

Retriever to become aggressive toward cats, other dogs, other humans, other wildlife, children riding by on bikes or skateboards, the mail carrier, or the people next door.
In addition, a dog that receives a fright or who is excited and forgets about the shock they are going to receive, may run through an electronic fence and then be too frightened or stressed to come back home because it means that they must pass through the painful barrier again.

Furthermore, it is actually possible that electronic fencing may encourage a dog to escape the yard simply because they associate their yard with pain. This feeling can be reinforced if a dog escapes the electronic yard and then is again punished by the shock when they attempt to come home.

Another factor to keep in mind with respect to electronic fencing is that other dogs or teasing children can freely enter the yard and torment or attack your dog, and a thief bent on stealing your designer Mini Golden will be able to do so with ease.

The absolute best way to keep your dog safe in their own yard, while helping to establish your role as guardian and leader, is to be out there with them while they are on leash, and to only permit them freedom in your yard under your close supervision.

Chapter 11: Medical Care & Safety

1. Choosing a Veterinarian

A consideration to keep in mind when choosing a veterinarian clinic will be that some clinics specialize in caring for smaller pets, and some specialize in larger animal care, while still others have a wide ranging area of expertise and will care for all animals, including livestock and reptiles.

Choosing a clinic will be a personal decision, however, your dog's needs may be better served by choosing a clinic that specializes in the care of smaller domesticated pets.

Choosing a good veterinary clinic will be very similar to choosing the right health care clinic or doctor for your own personal health because you want to ensure that your Miniature Golden Retriever puppy receives the quality care they deserve.

Begin your search by asking other dog owners where they take their furry friends and whether they are happy with the service they receive.

If you don't know anyone to ask, visit the local pet store in your area as they should be able to provide you with references and local listings of pet care clinics.

Next, check online, because a good pet clinic will have an active website up and running that will list details of all the services they provide along with an overview of all staff members, their education and qualifications.

Once you've narrowed your search, it's time to personally visit the clinics you may be interested in, as this will be a good opportunity for you to visually inspect the facility, interact with the staff and perhaps meet the veterinarians face to face.

Of course, it's not just you who needs to feel comfortable with the clinic chosen and those working there. Your puppy needs to feel comfortable, too, and this is where visiting a clinic and interacting with the staff and veterinarians will provide you with an idea of their experience and expertise in handling your puppy.

If your puppy is comfortable with them, then you will be much more likely to trust that they will be providing the best care for your puppy who will need to receive all their vaccinations and yearly check-ups, and eventually be spayed or neutered.

It's also a good idea to take your puppy into your chosen clinic several times before they actually need to be there for any treatment, so that they are not fearful of the new smells and unfamiliar surroundings.

2. Neutering and Spaying

While it can sometimes be difficult to find the definitive answer when asking when is the best time to neuter or spay your young Miniature Golden Retriever because there are varying opinions on this topic, one thing that most veterinarians do agree on is that earlier spaying or neutering, between 4 and 6 months of age, is a better choice than waiting.

Spaying or neutering surgeries are carried out under general anesthesia, and as more dogs are being neutered at younger ages, speak with your veterinarian and ask for their recommendations regarding the right age to spay or neuter your Miniature Golden Retriever, and following are some points to be aware of:

1) Effects on Aggression: intact (non-neutered) males and females are more likely to display aggression related to sexual behavior than are dogs that have been neutered or spayed.

Fighting, particularly in male dogs that is directed at other males, is less common after neutering, and the intensity of other types of aggression, such as irritable aggression in females will be totally eliminated by spaying.

While neutering or spaying is not a treatment for aggression, it can certainly help to minimize the severity and escalation of aggressiveness and is often the first step toward resolving an aggressive behavior problem.

2) What is Neutering? this surgical procedure is carried out by a licensed veterinarian surgeon to render a male dog unable to reproduce. In males, the surgery is also referred to as *"castration"* because the procedure entails the removal of the young dog's testicles.

When the testicles are removed, what is left behind is an empty scrotal sac (which used to contain the puppy's testicles) and this empty sac will soon shrink in size until it is no longer noticeable.

3) Neutering Males: neutering a male puppy before they are six months of age can help to ensure that they will be less likely to suffer from obesity problems when they grow older.

Neutering can also mean that a male Miniature Golden Retriever will be less likely to have the urge to wander.

Furthermore, waiting until a male Miniature Golden Retriever is older than six months before having them neutered could mean that they will experience the effects of raging testosterone that will drive them to escape their yards by any means necessary to search for females to mate with.

Non-neutered males also tend to spray or mark territory much more often, both inside and outside the home, and during this time can start to display aggressive tendencies toward other dogs as well as people.

4) What is Spaying? this surgical procedure (also called *"sterilization")* is carried out by a licensed veterinarian to prevent the female dog from becoming pregnant and to stop regular heat cycles.

The sterilization procedure is much more involved for a female puppy (than for a male), as it requires the removal of both ovaries and the uterus by incision into the puppy's abdominal cavity. The uterus is also removed during this surgery to prevent the possibility of it becoming infected later on in life.

5) Spaying Females: preferably, a female Miniature Golden Retriever puppy should be spayed before their very first estrus or heat cycle.

Females in heat often appear more agitated and irritable while sleeping and eating less and some may become extremely aggressive toward other dogs.

Spaying female puppies before their first heat pattern can eliminate these hormonal stressors and reduce the opportunity of mammary glandular tumors. Early spaying also protects against various other potential concerns, such as uterine infections.

6) Effects on General Temperament: many dog owners often become needlessly worried that a neutered or spayed dog will lose their vigor.

Rest assured that a dog's personality or energy level will not be modified or altered in any way by the neutering process, and in fact, many unfavorable qualities resulting from hormonal impact may resolve after surgery.

Your Mini Golden will certainly not come to be less caring or cheerful, and neither will he or she resent you because you are not denying your dog any essential encounters. You will, however, be acting as a conscientious, informed, and caring guardian.

There is little evidence to suggest that the nature of a female will improve after having a litter of puppies.

What is important is that you do not project your own psychological needs or concerns onto your puppy, because there is no gain to be had from permitting sexual activity in either male or female canines.

For instance, it is not *"abnormal"* or *"mean"* to manage a puppy's reproductive activity by having them sterilized. Rather, it is unkind and irresponsible not to neuter or spay a dog and there are many positive benefits of having this procedure carried out.

7) Effects on Escape and Roaming: a neutered or spayed dog is less likely to wander. Castrated male dogs have the tendency to patrol smaller sized outdoor areas and are less likely to participate in territorial conflicts with perceived opponents.

NOTE: a dog that has actually already experienced successful escapes from the yard may continue to wander after they are spayed or neutered.

8) Effects on Problem Elimination: an unsterilized dog may urinate or defecate inside the home or in other undesirable areas in an attempt to stake territorial claims, relieve anxiety, or advertise their available reproductive status.

While neutering or spaying a puppy after they have already begun to inappropriately eliminate or mark territory to announce their sexual availability to other dogs will reduce the more powerful urine odor as well as eliminate the hormonal factors, once this habit has begun, the undesirable behavior may continue to persist after neutering or spaying.

9) Possible Weight Gain: while metabolic changes that occur after spaying or neutering can cause some puppies to gain weight, often the real culprit for any weight gain is the human who feels guilty for subjecting their puppy to any kind of pain and therefore attempt to make themselves feel better by feeding more treats or meals to their companion.

If you are concerned about weight gain after neutering or spaying a puppy, simply adjust their food and treat consumption as needed and make sure that they receive adequate daily exercise.

It's a very simple process to change your dog's food intake according to their physical demands and how they look, and if your puppy's daily exercise and level of activity has not changed after they have been spayed or neutered, there will likely be no change in food management necessary.

10) Pediatric Spaying/Neutering: in the past, the usual time frame for neutering or spaying a puppy was between the ages of 5 and 6 months. However, even though there exists quite a bit of debate amongst veterinarians, pediatric spaying or neutering has become more widely accepted. The American Veterinary Medical Association has supported this concept of very early sterilization since 2004 in an effort to help reduce the numbers of homeless, unwanted animals.

Pediatric spaying or neutering is also called *"prepuberal"* or "early" spaying or neutering and may be carried out at a much earlier age, usually between 6 and 14 weeks.

3. Why Vaccinate a Puppy?

Puppies need to be vaccinated by a veterinarian in order to provide them with protection against four common and serious diseases referred to as ***"DAPP"***, which stands for **D**istemper, **A**denovirus, **P**arainfluenza and **P**arvo Virus.

Approximately one week after your puppy has completed all three sets of primary DAPP vaccinations they will be fully protected from those specific diseases. Thereafter, most veterinarians will recommend a once a year vaccination for the next year or two.

It has now become common practice to vaccinate adult dogs every three years, and if your veterinarian is insisting on a yearly vaccination for your puppy, you need to ask them why, because to do otherwise is considered by most professionals to be *"over vaccinating"*.

4. Common Diseases and Viruses

a) Distemper: is a contagious and serious viral illness for which there is currently no known cure.

This deadly virus, which is spread either through the air or by direct or indirect contact with a dog that is already infected or other distemper carrying wildlife, including ferrets, raccoons, foxes, skunks and wolves, is a relative of the measles virus that affects humans.

Canine distemper is sometimes also called *"hard pad disease"* because some strains of the distemper virus actually cause the thickening of the pads on a dog's feet, which can also affect the end of a dog's nose. In dogs or animals with weak immune systems, death may result two to five weeks after the initial distemper infection.

Early symptoms of distemper include fever, loss of appetite, and mild eye inflammation that may only last a day or two. Symptoms become more serious and noticeable as the disease progresses.

A puppy or dog that survives the distemper virus will usually continue to experience symptoms or signs of the disease throughout their remaining lifespan, including *"hard pad disease"* as well as *"enamel hypoplasia"*, which is damage to the enamel of the puppy's teeth that are not yet formed or that have not yet pushed through the gums. Enamel hypoplasia is caused when the distemper virus kills the cells that manufacture tooth enamel.

b) Adenovirus: causes infectious canine hepatitis, which can range in severity from very mild to very serious, sometimes resulting in death.

Symptoms can include coughing, loss of appetite, increased thirst and urination, tiredness, runny eyes and nose, vomiting, bruising or bleeding under the skin, swelling of the head, neck and body, fluid accumulation in the abdomen area, jaundice (yellow tinge to the skin), a bluish clouding of the cornea of the eye (called "hepatitis blue eye") and seizures.

There is no specific treatment for infectious canine hepatitis and treatment is focused on managing symptoms while the virus runs its course. In severe cases, hospitalization and intravenous fluid therapy may be required.

c) Canine Parainfluenza Virus (CPIV): also referred to as *"canine influenza virus"*, *"greyhound disease"* or *"race flu"*, which is easily spread through the air or by coming into contact with respiratory secretions, was originally a virus that only affected horses.

This disease is believed to have adapted to become contagious to dogs, is easily spread from dog to dog, and may cause symptoms that become fatal.

While the more frequent occurrences of this respiratory infection are seen in areas where there are high dog populations, such as race tracks, boarding kennels and pet stores, this virus is highly contagious to any dog or puppy at any age.

Symptoms can include a dry, hacking cough, difficulty breathing, wheezing, runny nose and eyes, sneezing, fever, loss of appetite, tiredness, depression and possible pneumonia. In cases where only a cough exists, tests will be required to determine whether the cause of the cough is the parainfluenza virus or the less serious *"kennel cough"*.

While many dogs can naturally recover from this virus, they will remain contagious, and for this reason, in order to prevent the spread to other animals, aggressive treatment of the virus with antibiotics and antiviral drugs will be the general course of action.

In more severe cases, a cough suppressant may be prescribed, as well as intravenous fluids to help prevent secondary bacterial infection.

d) Canine Parvovirus (CPV): is a highly contagious viral illness affecting puppies and dogs. Parvovirus also affects other canine species including foxes, coyotes and wolves.
There are two forms of this virus (1) the more common intestinal form, and (2) the less common cardiac form, which can cause death in young puppies.

Symptoms of the intestinal form of parvovirus include vomiting, bloody diarrhea, weight loss, and lack of appetite, while the less common cardiac form attacks the heart muscle.

Early vaccination in young puppies has radically reduced the incidence of canine parvovirus infection, which is easily transmitted either by direct contact with an infected dog, or indirectly, by sniffing an infected dog's feces.

The virus can also be brought into a dog's environment on the bottom of human shoes that may have stepped on infected feces, and there is evidence that this hardy virus can live in ground soil for up to a year.

Recovery from parvovirus requires both aggressive and early treatment. With proper treatment, death rates are relatively low (between 5 and 20%), although chances of survival for puppies are much lower than for older dogs, and in all instances, there is no guarantee of survival.

Treatment of parvovirus requires hospitalization where intravenous fluids and nutrients are administered to help combat dehydration. Antibiotics will be given to counteract secondary bacterial infections, and as necessary, medications to control nausea and vomiting may also be given.

Without prompt and proper treatment, dogs that have severe parvovirus infections can die within 48 to 72 hours.

5. Other Diseases and Viruses

1) Rabies: is a viral disease transmitted by coming into contact with the saliva of an infected animal, usually through a bite. The virus travels to the brain along the nerves and once symptoms develop, death is almost certainly inevitable, usually following a prolonged period of suffering.

If you plan to travel out of State or across country borders, you will need to make sure that your Miniature Golden Retriever has an up to date Rabies Vaccination Certificate (NASPHV form 51) indicating they have been inoculated against rabies.

Vaccinating dogs against rabies is also compulsory in most countries in mainland Europe, as is permanent identification and registration of dogs through the use of a Pet Passport.

Those living in a country that is rabies free (UK, Eire) are not required to vaccinate their dogs against rabies, unless they intend to travel.

2) Leishmaniasis: is caused by a parasite and is transmitted by a bite from a sand fly and there is no definitive answer for effectively combating Leishmaniasis, especially since one vaccine will not prevent the known multiple species.

In areas where the known cause is a sand fly, deltamethrin collars (containing a neurotoxic insecticide) worn by the dogs has been proven to be 86% effective. There are two types of Leishmaniasis: (1) a skin reaction causing hair loss, lesions and ulcerative dermatitis, and (2) a more severe, abdominal organ reaction, which is also known as *"black fever"*.

When the disease affects organs of the abdominal cavity the **symptoms** include loss of appetite, diarrhea, severe weight loss, exercise intolerance, vomiting, nosebleed, tarry feces, fever, pain in the joints, excessive thirst and urination and inflammation of the muscles.

Leishmaniasis spreads throughout the body to most organs, with kidney failure being the most common cause of death. Virtually all infected dogs develop this system wide disease and as much as 90% of those infected will also display skin reactions.

Affected dogs in the US are frequently found to have acquired this infection in another country.

Of note is that this disease is regularly found in the Middle East, the area around the Mediterranean basin, Portugal, Spain, Africa, South and Central America, southern Mexico and the US, with regular cases reported in Oklahoma and Ohio, where it is found in 20 to 40% of the dog population.

There have also been a few reported cases in Switzerland, northern France and the Netherlands.

NOTE: Leishmaniasis is a *"zoonotic"* infection, which is a contagious disease that can be spread between both animals and humans. This means that the organisms residing in the Leishmaniasis lesions can be communicated to humans.

Treatment in dogs is often difficult and the dog may suffer from relapses. Leishmaniasis poses a significant risk to the health of your dog, especially if you travel to the Mediterranean.

3) Lyme Disease: is one of the most common tick-borne diseases in the world, which is transmitted by Borrelia bacteria found in the deer or sheep tick. Lyme disease, also called *"borreliosis"*, is also a zoonotic disease that can affect both humans and dogs and this disease can be fatal.

The Borrelia bacteria that causes Lyme's disease is transmitted by slow-

feeding, hard-shelled deer or sheep ticks, and the tick usually has to be attached to the dog for a minimum of 18 hours before the infection is transmitted.
Symptoms of this disease in a young or adult dog include recurrent lameness from joint inflammation, loss of appetite, depression, stiff walk with arched back, sensitivity to touch, swollen lymph nodes, fever, kidney damage and rare heart or nervous system complications.

While Lyme disease has been reported in dogs throughout the United States and Europe, it is most prevalent in the upper Mid-Western states, the Atlantic seaboard, and the Pacific coastal states.

In order to properly diagnose and treat Lyme disease, blood tests will be required, and if the tests are positive, oral antibiotics will be prescribed to treat the conditions.

Prevention is the key to keeping this disease under control because dogs that have had Lyme disease before are still able to get the disease again. There is a vaccine for Lyme disease and dogs living in areas that have easy access to these ticks should be vaccinated yearly.

4) Rocky Mountain Spotted Fever (RMSF): is a tick-transmitted disease very often seen in dogs in the East, Midwest, and plains region of the US, and the organisms causing RMSF are transmitted by both the American dog tick and the RMSF tick, which must be attached to the dog for a minimum of five hours in order to transmit the disease.

Common symptoms of RMSF include fever, reduced appetite, depression, painful joints, lameness, vomiting and diarrhea.

Some dogs affected with RMSF may develop heart abnormalities, pneumonia, kidney failure, liver damage, or even neurological signs, such as seizures or unsteady, wobbly or stumbling gait. Diagnosis of this disease requires blood testing and if the results are positive, oral antibiotics will be given to the infected dog for approximately two weeks. Dogs that can clear the organism from their systems will recover and after being infected will remain immune to future infection.

5) Ehrlichiosis: a tick-borne disease transmitted by both the brown dog tick and the Lone Star Tick.

Ehrlichiosis has been reported in every state in the US, as well as worldwide. Common symptoms include depression, reduced appetite, fever, stiff and painful joints and bruising.

Signs of infection typically occur less than a month after a tick bite and last for approximately four weeks. There is no vaccine available.

Blood tests may be required to test for antibodies and treatment will require a course of antibiotics for up to four weeks in order to completely clear the organism from the infected dog's system.

After a dog has been previously infected, they may develop antibodies to the organism, but will not be immune to being re-infected.

Dogs living in areas of the country where the Ehrlichiosis tick disease are common or widespread may be prescribed low doses of antibiotics during tick season.

6) Anaplasmosis: deer ticks and Western blacklegged ticks are carriers of the bacteria that transmit canine Anaplasmosis. However, there is also another form of Anaplasmosis (caused by a different bacteria) that is carried by the brown dog tick.

Because the deer tick also carries other diseases, some animals may be at risk of developing more than one tick-borne disease at the same time. Signs of Anaplasmosis are similar to Ehrlichiosis and include painful joints, diarrhea, fever, and vomiting as well as possible nervous system disorders.

A dog will usually begin to show signs of Anaplasmosis within a couple of weeks after infection and diagnosis will require blood and urine testing, and sometimes other specialized laboratory tests.

Treatment is with oral antibiotics for up to 30 days, depending on how severe the infection may be. When this disease is quickly treated, most dogs will recover completely, however, subsequent immunity is not guaranteed, which means that a dog may be re-infected if exposed again.

7) Tick Paralysis: is caused when ticks attach themselves to a dog's skin and secrete a toxin that affects the dog's nervous system.
Affected dogs show signs of weakness and limpness approximately one week after being first bitten by ticks.

Symptoms usual begin with a change in pitch of the dog's usual bark, which will become softer, and weakness in the rear legs that eventually involves all four legs, which is then followed by the dog showing difficulty breathing and swallowing.

If the condition is not diagnosed and properly treated, death can occur. Treatment involves locating and removing the tick and then treating the infected dog with tick anti-serum.

8) Canine Coronavirus: while this highly contagious intestinal disease, which is spread through the feces of contaminated dogs, was first discovered in Germany during 1971 when there was an outbreak in sentry dogs, it is now found worldwide. This virus can be destroyed by most commonly available disinfectants.

Symptoms include diarrhea, vomiting and weight loss or anorexia.

While deaths resulting from this disease are rare, and treatment generally requires only medication to relieve the diarrhea, dogs that are more severely affected may require intravenous fluids to combat dehydration.

There is a vaccine available, which is usually given to puppies because they are more susceptible at a young age. This vaccine is also given to show dogs that have a higher risk of exposure to the disease.

9) Leptospirosis: is a disease that occurs throughout the world that can affect many different kinds of animals, including dogs, and as it is also a zoonotic disease, it can affect humans, too.

There is potential for both dogs and humans to die from this disease. The disease is always present in the environment, which makes it easy for any dog to pick up. This is because it is found in many common animals, such as rats, and wildlife, as well as domestic livestock.

Veterinarians generally see more cases of Leptospirosis in the late summer and fall, which is probably because that is when more pets and wildlife are out and about. More cases also occur after heavy rain falls. The disease is most common in mild or tropical climates around the World, and in the US or Canada it is more common in states or provinces that receive heavy rainfall.

The good news is that you can protect your dog from leptospirosis by vaccination, and while puppies are not routinely vaccinated against leptospirosis because chances of contracting the disease depend upon the lifestyle of the dog as well as the area in which the dog lives, it makes sense to vaccinate against this disease if you and your dog do live in an area considered a hot spot for leptospirosis, so ask your veterinarian.

City rat populations are a major carrier of leptospirosis. Cold winter conditions lower the risk because the leptospira organisms do not tolerate the freezing and thawing of near-zero temperatures. They are killed rapidly by drying, but they persist in standing water, dampness, mud and alkaline conditions.

Most of the infected wild animals and domestic animals that spread leptospirosis do not appear ill.

The leptospira take up residence in the kidneys of infected animals, which can include rats, mice, squirrels, skunks, and raccoons and when these animals void urine they contaminate their environment with living leptospira.

Dogs usually become infected after sniffing urine or by wading, swimming or drinking contaminated water that has infected urine in it, and this is how the disease passes from animal to animal. As well, the leptospira can also enter through a bite wound or if a dog eats infected material.

6. Additional Vaccinations

Depending upon where you and your Miniature Golden Retriever live, your veterinarian may suggest additional vaccinations to help combat diseases that may be more common in your area.

7. When Is a Puppy Vaccinated?

The first vaccination needle is normally given to a puppy around six to eight weeks of age, which means that generally it will be the responsibility of the Miniature Golden Retriever breeder to ensure that the puppy's first shots have been received before their new owner takes them home.

Thereafter, it will be the new puppy's guardians that will be responsible for ensuring that the next two sets of shots, which are usually given three to four weeks after each other, are given by the new guardian's veterinarian at the proper intervals.

8. De-Worming

De-worming kills internal parasites that your dog or puppy may have. The two most common types of worms that may infest your canine companion are round worms and tapeworms, both of which can be passed on to humans.

NOTE: even though your living conditions may be completely sanitary, it is still possible for your dog to have internal parasites because this has nothing to do with where you live or how clean you keep your dog and your home. It is recommended by the Center for Disease Control (CDC) that puppies be dewormed every 2 weeks until they are 3 months old, and then every month after that, in order to control worms.

Puppies are usually regularly wormed by the breeder before the puppies are taken to their homes, however, many veterinarians recommend worming dogs for tapeworm and roundworms every 6-12 months.

The health risks to your puppy or dog include diarrhea, vomiting, slow growth, and in serious cases a bowel blockage or pneumonia, even death.

Most puppies and dogs will experience worms at some stage in their life and thankfully the problem can be easily and swiftly eliminated with worming medication.

9. Special Care When Pregnant

As canine pregnancy lasts approximately 63 days, and a female will go into labor within 56 to 66 days after becoming pregnant.

Immediately upon noticing signs of pregnancy you will want to take your dog to your veterinarian to confirm the pregnancy and to receive instructions for the proper feeding and care.

During the first days of pregnancy your Miniature Golden Retriever may experience morning sickness. Your veterinarian may recommend increasing food intake or adding an egg or cottage cheese to your dog's meals and switching to puppy kibble, which is higher in protein, at around the 30 day mark.

As the female becomes heavier with the puppies, she will lose interest in exercising and her other normal activities and will need to sleep more.

When the time for birthing is drawing near, the Miniature Golden Retriever female will start to display "nesting" characteristics where she will search for a warm and safe place to give birth.
You can help by providing a nesting box and she will likely want to take things into the box to make it more comfortable, such as towels or even a stuffed toy that she will begin to mother.

When the time draws near to whelping, the female may completely lose her appetite and show distress by pacing, panting, and acting uncomfortable.

When the birthing time is near, the dog's temperature needs to be checked, and should be around 100.2 to 100.8 degrees Fahrenheit (37.89 to 38.22 degrees Centigrade).

When her temperature drops to approximately 98 to 99.4 degrees Fahrenheit (36.67 to 37.44 degrees Centigrade), the puppies will usually be born within 24 hours.

If you are at all worried about the birthing process you will want to take the mother Miniature Golden Retriever immediately to your veterinarian's office.

If all goes well at home, within 5-6 hours of the last puppy's birth, you will need to take the mother and her puppies to your veterinarian for a check-up to make sure that she has birthed all puppies and placentas, and that the puppies are all healthy.

10. Licensing

Many cities and jurisdictions around the world require that dogs be licensed.

Usually a dog license is an identifying tag that the dog will be required to wear on their collar. The tag will have an identifying number and a contact number for the registering organization, so that if someone finds a lost dog wearing a tag, the owner of the dog can be contacted.

Most dog tags are only valid for one year, and will need to be renewed annually at the beginning of every New Year. This involves paying a fee, which can vary from jurisdiction to jurisdiction.

From one extreme to the next, owners of dogs living in Beijing, China must pay a licensing fee of $600 (£360), while those living in Great Britain require no fee, because the licensing of dogs was abolished in 1987.

Ireland and Northern Ireland both require dogs to be licensed and in Germany dog ownership is taxed, rather than requiring licensing, with higher taxes being paid for breeds of dogs deemed to be "dangerous".

Most US states and municipalities have licensing laws in effect and Canadian, Australian and New Zealand dogs also must be licensed, with the yearly fee approximately $30 to $50 (£18 to £30) depending upon whether the dog has been spayed or neutered.

11. Pet Insurance

Pet guardians commonly ask themselves, when considering medical insurance for their dog, whether they can afford not to have it.

On the one hand, in light of all the new treatments and medications that are now available for our dogs, that usually come with a very high price tag, an increasing number of guardians have decided to add pet insurance to their list of monthly expenses.

On the other hand, some humans believe that placing money into a savings account, in case unforeseen medical treatments are required, makes more sense.

Pet insurance coverage can cost anywhere from $2,000 to $6,000 USD (£1,201 to £3,604) over an average lifespan of a dog, and unless your dog is involved in a serious accident, or contracts a life-threatening disease, you may never need to pay out that much for treatment.

Whether you decide to start a savings account for your Miniature Golden Retriever so that you will always have funds available for unforeseen health issues, or you decide to buy a health insurance plan, most dog lovers will go to any lengths to save the life of their beloved companions.

Having access to advanced technological tools and procedures means that our dogs are now being offered treatment options that were once only reserved for humans.

Now, some canine conditions that were once considered fatal are being treated at considerable costs ranging anywhere between $1,000 and $5,000

(£597 and £2,986) or more.

However, even in the face of rapidly increasing costs of caring for our dogs, owners purchasing pet insurance remain a small minority.

In an effort to increase the numbers of people buying pet insurance, insurers have teamed with the American Kennel Club and Petco Animal Supplies to offer the insurance, and more than 1,600 companies, such as Office Depot and Google, offer pet insurance coverage to their employees as an optional employee benefit.

Even though you might believe that pet insurance will be your savior anytime your dog needs a trip to the vet's office, you really need to be careful when considering an insurance plan, because there are many policies that contain small print excluding certain ages, hereditary or chronic conditions.

Unfortunately, most people don't consider pet insurance when their pets are healthy because buying pet insurance means playing the odds, and unless your dog becomes seriously ill, you end up paying for something that may never happen. However, just like car insurance, you can't buy it after you've had that accident.

For instance, if you take your dog to your veterinarian who discovers that they have something wrong with their eyes, and then you decide to purchase insurance (because you will be required to give the insuring company a history of your dog's health) the eye issue will be part of the history and will likely be excluded from your insurance policy.

In other words, if you're planning on purchasing health insurance for your dog, do it before any problems arise in order to avoid having conditions that may present themselves in the future from being excluded from your policy.

As well, you need to keep in mind that canine health insurance rates will likely increase as your dog gets older. When your dog is younger, while your policy may only be $17 (£10) per month, it may increase considerably to as much as $170 (£100) or more per month as your dog becomes middle or senior aged, at around 8 to 10 years of age.

Since many of us, in today's uncertain economy, may be hard pressed to pay a high veterinarian bill, and generally speaking, the alternative of paying monthly pet insurance premiums will provide peace of mind and improved veterinarian care for our best friends.

Shop around, because as with all insurance policies, pet insurance policies will vary greatly between companies and the only way to know for certain exactly what sort of coverage you are buying is to be holding a copy of that policy in your hand so that you can clearly read what will and what will not be covered.

Don't forget to carefully read the fine print to avoid any nasty surprises, because the time to discover that a certain procedure will not be covered is not when you are in the middle of filing a claim.

Before Purchasing a Policy

There are several considerations to be aware of before choosing to purchase a pet insurance policy, including:

- Is your dog required to undergo a physical exam?
- Is there a waiting period before the policy becomes active?
- What percentage of the bill does the insurance company pay?
- Are payments limited or capped in any way?
- Are there co-pays (cost to you up front)?
- Does the plan cover pre-existing conditions?
- Does the plan cover chronic or recurring medical problems?
- Can you choose any vet or animal hospital to treat your pet?
- Are prescription medications covered?
- Are you covered when traveling with your pet?
- Does the policy pay if your pet is being treated and then dies?

When you love your dog and worry that you may not have the funds to cover an emergency medical situation that could unexpectedly cost thousands, the right pet insurance policy will provide both peace of mind and better health care for your beloved fur friend.

12. Identifying and Finding Lost Dogs

a) Micro-Chipping: this implant is a very small integrated circuit, approximately twice the size of a grain of rice, enclosed in glass that is implanted underneath the dog's skin (or other animal) with a syringe. The chip uses passive Radio Frequency Identification (RFID) technology, and is also known as a PIT tag (Passive Integrated Transponder).

The microchip is usually implanted, without anesthetic, into the scruff of a dog's neck by a veterinarian or shelter and has no internal power source, which means that they must be read by a scanner or *"interrogator"* that energizes the capacitor in the chip, which then sends radio signals back to the scanner so that the identifying number can be read.

Manufacturers of microchips often donate scanners to animal shelters and veterinarian clinics and hospitals.

While many communities are proposing making micro-chipping of all dogs mandatory, such as N. Ireland, and micro-chipping is a requirements for any dogs traveling to the state of Hawaii, many others are not especially pleased with this idea because they believe it's just more big business for little reward. For instance, while approximately one quarter of European dogs have a microchip implant, the idea is definitely lacking in popularity in the United States, where only 5% of dogs are micro-chipped.

Even though micro-chipping is used by animal shelters, pounds, animal control officers, breeders and veterinarians in order to help return a higher percentage of lost canines to their owners, some of the resistance to this idea can be explained by inherent problems with the ability of some organizations to correctly read the implants.

As an example, if the scanner is not tuned to the same frequency as the implanted microchip, it will not be read, which renders the process useless.

Pet microchips are manufactured with different frequencies, including 125 kHz, 128 kHz and 134.2 kHz. While approximately 98% of the pet microchips in the US use 125 kHz, those in Europe use 134.2 kHz.

In other words, if the facility reading your dog's microchip does not have a compatible scanner, your dog will not be identified and returned to you.

Further, what may turn out to be worse than the scanner incompatibility problem could be increasing evidence to indicate that microchips might cause Cancer.

As well, some microchips will migrate inside the dog's body and while they may start out in the dog's neck, they could end up in their leg or some other body part.

You will have to weigh information known about microchips, including possible Cancer risks, and the odds of losing your dog against whether or not a microchip is something you want to have for your Mini Golden. Whether or not you choose a microchip for your dog, generally the cost ranges between $25 and $50 (£15 and £30) depending on what your veterinarian may charge for this service.

NOTE: as of 6th April 2017, it is mandatory for those owning dogs in the UK to have them micro-chipped.

b) Tattooing: dogs are tattooed to help identify them in case they are lost or stolen. Many dog guardians prefer this safe, simple solution to micro-chipping because there is no need to locate a scanner that reads the correct frequency and there are no known side effects.

Because a tattoo is visible, it is immediately recognizable and reported when a lost dog is found, which means that tattooing could easily be the most effective means of identification available. As well, dog thieves are less likely to steal a dog that has a permanent visible form of identification. There are several registries for tattooed dogs, including the National Dog Tattoo Registry in the UK, which has a network of Accredited Tattooists across the UK.

The fee for tattooing and registering a dog for their lifetime is approximately $42.52 (£24.98).

In the United States, the National Dog Registry (NDR) was founded in 1966 and since then, NDR has supervised, directed, conducted, or overseen the tattooing of more than 6 million animals.

The cost for tattooing a single dog is approximately $10 (£5.90), and you will also have to pay a one-time registration fee of $45 (£26.44).

c) Pet Trackers: in today's electronic world, many people are wondering if a Pet Tracker might be a good idea for helping to keep their beloved canine safe. So, what exactly are Pet Trackers, how much do they cost, how do they work and how do you know which one to choose? First of all, you need to know that there are many in the marketplace and that there are basically two categories comprised of (1) Cellular GPS Trackers and (2) Radio Trackers, which are a special collar attached to your dog.

A GPS Tracker can help you locate your dog in real time by utilizing cellular towers and requires the use of a SIM card or some sort of cellular service, with average pricing ranging from $100 (£77) to $300 (£231).

Radio Trackers, which have been used for decades, utilize what some may consider outdated technology and are often used for hunting dogs, functioning over a limited range, much like a "Walkie Talkie". The more you spend for a Radio Tracker, the greater the range will be and pricing can range from $200 (£154) to $1,000 (£770).

d) Where to Look: if your dog goes missing, there are many places you can contact and steps you can take that may help you locate your lost dog, including:

- Retracing your dog's last known location;
- Contacting your friends and neighbors;
- Putting up flyers on telephone poles throughout your neighborhood, with your contact details and your dog's photo;
- Calling all local shelters and pounds every day;
- Contacting local rescue organizations;
- Contacting your breeder;
- Contacting local schools - children might have seen your dog in their neighborhood;
- Distributing flyers with a photograph of your dog and your contact details in all neighborhood stores and businesses;
- Contacting all businesses that deal with lost pets;
- Posting a picture on your Facebook or other social media;
- Asking your local radio station for help;
- Advertising in your local newspaper.

13. Yearly Cost of Ownership

It can be difficult to accurately estimate what the cost of owning every Miniature Golden Retriever might be because there are too many variables and unexpected medical problems that may not otherwise be considered average.

For instance, you may like to buy fancy clothes, new collars and leashes every year, the latest toys and gadgets, or the most expensive food for your dog every week that might also not be considered average.
However, when thinking about sharing your life with a dog, it's important to consider more than just the daily cost of feeding your Miniature Golden Retriever. Many humans do not think about whether or not they can truly

afford to care for a dog before they bring one home, and not being prepared can cause stress and problems later on.

Remember that being financially responsible for your Miniature Golden Retriever is a large part of being a good guardian. Beyond the initial investment of purchasing your puppy from a reputable breeder, for most guardians, owning a Miniature Golden Retriever will include the costs associated with the following:

- Food
- Treats
- Pee pads, poop bags, potty patches
- Leashes and collars & safety harnesses for travel
- Travel kennels
- Potty training pens
- Clothing
- Toys
- Beds
- Professional grooming or equipment
- Shampoo and conditioner
- Neutering or spaying
- Regular veterinary care
- Obedience or dog whispering classes
- Pet sitting, walking or boarding
- Pet insurance
- Tattooing or Micro-chipping
- Yearly licensing
- Unexpected emergencies

As you can see from the list above, there are many variables involved in being a canine guardian that may or may not apply to your particular situation.

For instance, depending upon where you shop, what type of food and how much you feed your Miniature Golden Retriever, what sort of veterinarian or grooming care you choose, whether or not you have pet insurance and what types of items you purchase for your dog's well being, the yearly cost of owning a Miniature Golden Retriever could be estimated at anywhere between $700 and $3,000 (£420 and £1,800).
Other contributing factors that may have an effect on the overall yearly cost of owning a Miniature Golden Retriever can include the region where you live, the weather, the accessibility of the items you need, your own

lifestyle preferences and your dog's age and individual needs.

NOTE: another interesting fact that may influence the overall cost associated with caring for a particular breed of dog is, according to a recent study of 2,000 dogs, closely related to what breed of dog you may be sharing your home with.

According to a recent article written by Sarah Griffiths and published in the Daily Mail on June 13, 2014, there is now a list of the top ten most *"destructive"* purebred dog breeds.

This interesting study was carried out in reference to damage a dog may cause by ripping up the carpet, chewing through the fence, destroying the plants in the garden, eating the remote or your most expensive shoes, etc.

Of course, we expect some degree of damage from our furry friends during their lifetime, however, sometimes it can be quite a surprisingly large amount when you begin to add up the total amounts spent on cleaning, replacing and repairing damaged property, and the amount can be even higher if your dog becomes involved in destroying the neighbor's property, too.

The prize for the top ten destroyers is awarded to the cute and tiny Chihuahua, with average repair costs totaling $1,468 (£866) over the dog's lifetime, followed by the Dachshund, Boxer, Dalmatian, Bulldog, Great Dane, Husky, Beagle, Pointer and German Shepard.

On the other hand, the top ten least destructive breeds, in descending order, include such candidates as the Staffordshire Bull Terrier, causing a reported $302 (£178) of damage over the dog's lifetime, followed by the West Highland White Terrier, Yorkshire Terrier, Spaniel, Whippet, Shih Tzu, Labrador, Jack Russell, Rottweiler and Sheepdog.

With all the cross breeding and creation of hybrid, designer canines these days, there are some very interesting studies being carried out, such as this one, that will help us better understand our companions and what we may be letting ourselves in for.

NOTE: the more popular a particular breed may be, and the more positive traits that breed may enjoy will also make the cost of initially purchasing a puppy from a breeder more costly.

Chapter 12: Grooming

You will want to get your Miniature Golden puppy used to the routine of simple grooming early on so that they will not be traumatized for the rest of their life every time grooming is necessary.

Not taking the time to regularly involve your puppy in grooming sessions could lead to serious, unwanted behavior that may include trauma to your dog, not to mention stress or injury to yourself in the form of biting and scratching, that could result in a lifetime of unhappy grooming sessions.

When you neglect regular, daily or at least a weekly at home grooming session with your puppy or dog to remove dead hair and check toenails, this will not only cost you and your canine companion in terms of possible trauma, it may also cost you in veterinarian fees should you not be aware of a problem that could have been discovered early on during regular grooming sessions.

An effective home regimen should include not just surface brushing, but also getting to all those sensitive areas easily missed around the ears and collar area, the armpit area, and the back end and tail.

Do not allow yourself to get caught in the *"my dog doesn't like it"* trap, which is an excuse many owners will use to avoid regular grooming sessions.

When you allow your dog to dictate whether they will permit a grooming session, you are setting a dangerous precedent that could lead to a lifetime of trauma for both you and your dog.

When humans neglect daily grooming routines, many dogs develop a heightened sensitivity, especially with regard to having their legs and feet held, their ears inspected, or their nails clipped, and will do anything they can to avoid the process when you need to groom them.

Make a pact with yourself right from the first day you bring your puppy home never to neglect a regular grooming routine and not to avoid sensitive areas, such as regular brushing, trimming toenails or brushing teeth, just because your dog may not particularly *"like"* it.

Remember that a few minutes of regular grooming sessions each day with your Miniature Golden Retriever is also a wonderful opportunity for bonding.

1. Bath Time

Step One: before you get your dog or puppy anywhere near the water, it's important to make sure that you brush out any debris, dead hair, mats or tangles from their coat before you begin the bathing process.

As well, removing any debris or mats from your dog's coat beforehand will make the entire process easier on both you, your dog, and your drains, which will become clogged with dead hair if you don't remove it beforehand.

Step Two: whether you're bathing your dog or puppy in your bathtub or shower, you will always want to first lay down a rubber bath mat to provide a more secure footing for your dog and to prevent your tub or sink from being scratched.

Step Three: have everything you need for the bath (shampoo, conditioner, sponge, towels) right next to the tub or in the shower, so you don't have to go searching once your dog is already wet.

TIP

PLACE COTTON balls in your dog's ear canals to prevent accidental splashes from entering the ear canal that could later cause an ear infection.

Step Four: if using a tub, fill it with four to six inches of lukewarm water (not too hot as dogs are more sensitive to hot water than us humans) and put your Miniature Golden Retriever in the water. Completely wet your dog's coat right down to the skin by using a detachable showerhead. If you don't have a spray attachment, a cup or pitcher will work just as well.

TIP

NO DOG likes to have water poured over its head and into its eyes, so use a wet sponge or wash cloth to wet the head area.

Step Five: apply shampoo as indicated on the bottle instructions by beginning at the head and working your way down the back. Be careful not to get shampoo in the eyes, nose, mouth or ears. Comb the shampoo lather through your dog's hair with your fingers, making sure you don't miss the areas under the legs and tail.

Step Six: after allowing the shampoo to remain in your dog's coat for a couple of minutes, thoroughly rinse the Miniature Golden Retriever's coat, right down to the skin with clean, lukewarm water using the spray attachment, cup or pitcher. Comb through your dog's coat with your fingers to make sure all shampoo residue has been completely rinsed away.

TIP

ANY SHAMPOO remaining in a dog's coat will lead to irritation and itching. Once you've rinsed, take the time to rinse again, especially in the armpits and underneath the tail area.

Use your hands to gently squeeze all excess water from your dog's coat.

Step Seven: apply conditioner as indicated on the bottle instructions and work the conditioner throughout your dog's coat. Leave the conditioner in your dog's coat for two minutes and then thoroughly rinse again with warm water, unless the conditioner you are using is a *"leave-in"*, no-rinse formula.

NOTE: The best conditioner for a Miniature Golden Retriever will contain mink oil, which adds a gloss to deepen and enrich the natural color of the coat.

It is also a good idea to choose a brand of conditioner that contains sunscreen to help protect from ultraviolet radiation when your dog is outside on sunny days.

Applying a good conditioner containing protein to your Miniature Golden Retriever's coat after bathing will help to rebuild, restructure and protect the coat by bonding to the shaft of each individual hair.

Pull the plug on your tub and let the water drain away as you use your hands to squeeze excess water from your dog's legs and feet.

Step Eight: immediately out of the water, wrap your Miniature Golden Retriever in dry towels so they don't get cold and use the towels to gently squeeze out extra water before you allow them to shake and spray water

everywhere.
Unless it's a warm day out, you will want to dry your dog or puppy right away with your hand held hairdryer and be careful not to let the hot air get too close to their skin.

TIP

YOU CAN use your hand or a soft brush or comb to lift and fluff the coat to help it dry more quickly, and you will want to place your hand between the hairdryer and your Miniature Golden Retriever's hair so that they will never get a direct blast of hot air and never blow air directly into their face or ears.

Don't forget to remove the cotton balls from their ears and make sure the ears are dry.

2. Ear Care

There are many ear cleaning creams, drops, oils, rinses, solutions and wipes formulated for cleaning your dog's ears that you can purchase from your local pet store or veterinarian's office.

You may prefer to use a home remedy that will just as efficiently clean your Miniature Golden Retriever's ears, such as Witch Hazel or a 50:50 mixture of hydrogen peroxide and purified water.

TIP

If you are going to make your own ear cleaning solution, find a bottle with a nozzle, measure your solution, properly diluted and mixed into the bottle, and use your preparation to saturate a cotton makeup remover pad to wipe out the visible part of your dog's ears. Always make sure the ears are totally dried after cleaning.

3. Eye Care

Every dog should have their eyes regularly wiped with a warm, damp cloth to remove the build up of daily secretions in the corners of the eyes that can be unattractive and uncomfortable for the dog as the hair becomes glued together. If this build up is not removed every day, it can quickly become a cause of bacterial yeast growth that can lead to eye infections.

When you take a moment every day to gently wipe your dog's eyes with a warm, moist cloth, you will help to keep your dog's eyes comfortable and infection free.

4. Nail Care

Allowing your Miniature Golden Retriever to have long, untrimmed nails can result in various health hazards including infections or an irregular and uncomfortable gait that can result in damage to their skeleton.

Although most dogs do not particularly enjoy the process of having their nails trimmed, and most humans find the exercise to be a little scary, regular nail trimming is a very important grooming practice that should never be overlooked.

When you get them used to having their nails trimmed at a young age, they will quietly tolerate the process for the rest of their life. In order to keep your adult dog's toenails in good condition and the proper length, you will need to purchase a plier-type nail trimmer at a pet store and learn how to correctly use it.

Generally speaking, if you can hear your dog's nails clacking or scratching on the floor or road surface when they walk, their nails are too long, and if you continue to allow your dog's nails to be too long the nail quick will grow longer into the nail, which will make it more difficult to keep them trimmed to the correct length.

NOTE: when your Mini Golden is a small puppy, you may find it easier to trim their nails with a pair of nail scissors, which you can purchase at any pet store, that are smaller and less cumbersome to use on puppy nails and all you need to do is snip off the curved tip of each nail.

Further, if you want your dog's nails to be smooth, without the sharp edges clipping alone can create, you will also want to invest in a toenail file or a special, slow speed, rotary Dremel™ trimmer, equipped with a sanding disk, which is designed especially for dog nails.

Some dogs will prefer the rotary trimmer to the squeezing sensation of the nail clipper and when you keep your dog's nails regularly trimmed, the Dremel™ may be the only tool you will ever need.

NOTE: never use a regular Dremel™ tool on a dog's toenails as it will be too high speed and will burn your dog's toenails. Only use a slow speed Dremel™, Model 7300-PT Pet Nail Grooming Tool.

5. Dental Care

As a conscientious Miniature Golden Retriever guardian you will need to regularly care for your dog's teeth throughout their entire life.

a) Retained Primary Teeth: often a young dog will not naturally lose their puppy or baby teeth without intervention from a licensed veterinarian.

Therefore, keep a close watch on your puppy's teeth around the age of 6 or 7 months of age to make certain that the baby teeth have fallen out and that the adult teeth have space to grow in.

If your puppy has not naturally lost all their baby teeth, any remaining teeth will need to be pulled in order to allow room for the adult teeth to properly grow in, and the best time to do this will be the same time as they visit the veterinarian's office to be spayed or neutered.

b) Periodontal Disease: please be aware that 80% of three-year-old dogs suffer from periodontal disease and bad breath because their guardians do <u>not</u> look after their dog's teeth. What makes this shocking statistic even worse is that with simple, daily care it is possible to entirely prevent canine gum disease and bad breath.

The pain associated with periodontal disease will make your dog's life miserable, as it will be painful for them to eat and the associated bacteria can infect many parts of the dog's body, including the heart, kidney, liver and brain, all of which they will have to suffer in silence.

If your dog has bad breath, this could be the first sign of an unhealthy mouth and gum disease caused by plaque build-up on the teeth.

As well, if your dog is drooling excessively, this may be a symptom secondary to dental disease. Your dog may be experiencing pain or the salivary glands may be reacting to inflammation from excessive bacteria in the mouth.

If you notice your Mini Golden drooling, and it's not because they're anticipating that steak you've got grilling on the barbecue, you will want to

have them professionally examined at your veterinarian's office.
c) Teeth Brushing: slowly introduce your Miniature Golden Retriever to teeth brushing early on in their young life so that they will not fear it.

Begin with a finger cap toothbrush when they are young puppies, and then move to a soft bristled toothbrush, or even an electric brush, as all you have to do is hold it against the teeth while the brush does all the work. Sometimes with a manual brush, you may brush too hard and cause the gums to bleed.

Never use human toothpaste or mouthwash on your dog's teeth because dogs cannot spit and human toothpaste that contains toxic fluoride will be swallowed. There are many flavored dog toothpastes available at the pet store or veterinarian's office.

Also, it's a good idea to get your dog used to the idea of occasionally having their teeth scraped or scaled, especially the back molars which tend to build up plaque. Be very careful if you are doing this yourself because the tools are sharp.

TIP

IF YOU need help keeping your dog's mouth open while you do a quick brush or scrape, get yourself a piece of hard material (rubber or leather) that they can bite down on, so that they cannot fully close their mouth while you work on their teeth.

When your dog is a young puppy, take the time to get them used to having their mouth handled and your fingers rubbing their teeth and gums.

Next, buy some canine toothpaste at your local pet store specially flavored to appeal to dogs and apply this to your dog's teeth with your finger.

Then slowly introduce the manual or electric toothbrush to your Miniature Golden Retriever. When you go slowly, they will get used to the buzzing and vibrating of the electric brush, which will do a superior job of cleaning their teeth.

First, let them see the electric brush, then let them hear it buzzing, and before you put it in their mouth, let them feel the buzzing sensation on their body, while you move it slowly toward their head and muzzle.
When your Miniature Golden Retriever will allow you to touch their muzzle while the brush is turned on, the next step is to lift their lip and

quickly brush a couple of teeth at a time until they get used to having them all brushed at the same time.

Always happily praise them for allowing you to brush their teeth, especially when they are first getting used to the idea.

TIP

ANOTHER simple home solution for helping to keep your dog's breath fresh and their teeth white is Bicarbonate of Soda (baking soda). Simply sprinkle some into a dish and dip your finger or toothbrush first in water and then into the Bicarbonate of Soda. Then use this to clean your dog's teeth and massage their gums. Some dogs seem to object less to this procedure when you use your finger.

Whether you let the electric toothbrush do the work for you, or you are using your finger or a manual toothbrush, make certain that you brush in a circular motion and when using a brush, angle the bristles so that they extend underneath the gums to help prevent plaque buildup, gum disease and loose teeth.

d) Teeth Scaling: use of a tooth scraper or scaling tool once or twice a month can help to remove plaque buildup. Most accumulation will be found on the outside of the teeth and on the back molars, near or underneath the gum line. Go slowly and carefully because these tools are sharp and only do this when your dog is calm and relaxed, a little bit at a time.

e) Healthy Teeth Tips: despite what most dog owners might put up with as normal, it is not normal for your dog to have smelly dog breath or canine halitosis.

Bad breath is the first sign of an unhealthy mouth, which could involve gum disease or tooth decay. The following tips will help keep your dog's mouth and teeth healthy:

TIP

Hydrogen Peroxide – keep your dog's teeth sparkling white and their breath fresh by using old-fashioned hydrogen peroxide as your doggy toothpaste. Hydrogen peroxide is what's in the human whitening toothpaste. There will be such a small amount on the brush that it will not harm your dog, and will kill any bacteria in your dog's mouth.

Toothpaste – many canine toothpastes are formulated with active enzymes to help keep tartar build-up at bay.

Plaque and Halitosis – help prevent tooth plaque and doggy halitosis by feeding your dog natural, hard bones at least once a month, which will also help to remove tartar while polishing and keeping their teeth white.

Bones – feed large bones so there is no danger of swallowing, and do NOT boil the bones first because this makes the bone soft (which defeats the purpose of removing plaque), and boiling could cause bones to splinter into smaller pieces that could create a choking or puncturing hazard for your dog.

Dental Chews – feed a daily dental chew or hard biscuit to help to remove tartar while exercising the jaws and massaging the gums. Some dental chews contain natural breath freshening cinnamon, cloves or chlorophyll.

Coconut Oil – helps to prevent smelly dog breath while giving your dog's digestive, immune and metabolic functions a boost at the same time. Dogs love the taste, so add ¼ teaspoon to your dog's dinner and their breath will soon be much sweeter.

Teeth Brushing – keep your dog's mouth comfortable and healthy by getting into the habit of brushing their teeth every night before bedtime.

6. Skin Care

Keeping your dog's coat clean by regularly bathing with canine shampoo and conditioner and free from mats, debris and parasites, as well as providing plenty of clean water and feeding them a high quality diet free from allergy-causing ingredients will go a long way toward keeping their skin healthy and itch-free and their coat shiny and healthy looking.

Between bath times, there are many moist doggy wipes on the market that are especially formulated with the correct pH balance to help keep your dog clean and their skin healthy. Consider getting into the habit of wiping down your dog with one of these moist towels every night before bed.

7. Pest Control

a) Fleas: every dog usually picks up a flea or two sometime in their lifetime, so you should be prepared for this inevitability by ensuring that you always have a good flea shampoo on hand. If you notice your dog biting, scratching or chewing at his or herself, the chances that they have picked up a flea or two is quite high, so it's time for a flea bath.

b) Ticks: if your dog goes roaming freely through wooded and bushy areas with large trees, they may also pick up the occasional tick and you will have to carefully check.

Always carefully check through your dog's coat and ears after they have been romping through the woods, and make sure that you also have a solution on hand that will kill a tick or the proper tool that can easily and safely twist any size of tick out of a dog's skin.

A very effective product, which is 100% safe for humans and animals, that will kill ticks on contact, is a natural pest control product made by CedarCide called *"Best Yet Organic Bug Spray"*.

Ticks can also be quickly and easily removed with a simple to use *"Tick Twister"*.

8. Brushing & Combing

An often over looked task, that is a necessary part of maintaining the health of a dog, is daily brushing and combing.

As well, taking time to brush and comb your dog's coat will also give you an opportunity to bond with your dog, while identifying any problems (such as fatty lumps or bumps and matted hair) early on, before they may become more serious.

Make sure that your grooming sessions are as pleasant as possible by choosing the right tools for a Miniature Golden Retriever and their type and length of coat. You will need minimal brushes and combs to keep your dog's coat in good condition, including a slicker brush and a bristle brush.

As well as one or two brushes, and a comb, it's always a good idea to invest in a mat splitter, a rake and a flea comb.

9. Equipment Required

A **slicker brush** has short, thin, wire bristles arranged closely together and anchored to a flat, often rectangular, surface that's attached to a handle.

A slicker brush is an ideal grooming tool for helping to remove mats and tangles from a dog that has a longer coat. Slicker brushes are often used as a finishing brush after brushing with the bristle brush to smooth the dog's coat and create a shiny finish.

A **bristle brush** can be used to help remove debris and dead hair from the coat and also to help distribute natural oils to keep the coat looking healthy and shiny.

A **metal comb** can also be used for grooming a Miniature Golden Retriever. Most metal combs have a combination of widely spaced and narrow spaced teeth and are designed so that if you run into a tangle, you can switch to the wider spaced teeth while you work it out, without pulling and irritating your dog.

NOTE: Some combs have rotating teeth which makes the process of removing tangles from your dog's coat much easier on them without the pain of pulling and snagging.

Mat splitters are, as the name suggests, designed to split apart matted fur or hair so that you can then comb out the areas. Mats can quickly occur underneath the belly, in the armpits and tail area or around the neck.

A rake (which looks like a tiny rake) is very helpful for removing dead hair when your puppy is changing from their puppy coat to the new adult coat or during twice yearly molting when the dog may blow their undercoat.

Flea combs, as the name suggests, are designed for the specific purpose of removing fleas from a dog's coat.

A flea comb is usually small in size for maneuvering in tight spaces, and may be made of plastic or metal with the teeth of the comb placed very close together to trap hiding fleas.

A **Tick Twister**, is a simple device for painlessly, easily and quickly removing ticks that have imbedded themselves in your dog's skin.

Nail clippers or scissors (and/or a slow speed pet Dremel™) will be tools you need to use every couple of weeks or more, depending on how quickly your dog's nails grow and what types of surfaces they may be walking on.

10. Products

Shampoos: NEVER make the mistake of using human shampoo or conditioner for bathing your Miniature Golden Retriever because dogs have a different pH balance than humans.

For example, shampoo for humans has a pH balance of 5.5, whereas shampoo formulated for our canine companions has an almost neutral pH balance of 7.5.

Any shampoo with a lower pH balance will be harmful to your dog because it will be too harshly acidic for their coat and skin, which can create skin problems.

Always purchase a shampoo for your dog that is specially formulated to be gentle and moisturizing on your dog's coat and skin, that will not strip the natural oils, and which will nourish the coat to give it a healthy shine.

As a general rule, make sure that you read the instructions provided on the shampoo bottle, and avoid shampoos containing insecticides or harsh chemicals.

TIP

If your dog is suffering from an infestation of fleas, you may want to bathe them with shampoo containing pyrethrum (a botanical extract found in small, white daisies) or a shampoo containing citrus or tea tree oil, or bath and spray them with the very effective CedarCide products which can also be used to spray down their bedding and any carpets in the home.

Conditioners: while many of us use conditioner after we shampoo our own hair, a large number of canine guardians forget to use conditioner on our own dog's coat after bathing. Even if the bathing process is one that you wish to complete as quickly as possible, you will want to reconsider this little oversight because, just as conditioning our human hair improves its condition, the same is true for our dog's coat.

Conditioning your dog's coat will not only make it look and feel better, conditioning will also add additional benefits, including:

- Preventing the escape of natural oils and moisture
- Keeping the coat cleaner for a longer period of time
- Repairing a coat that has become damaged or dry

- Restoring a soft, silky feel
- Helping the coat dry more quickly
- Protection from the heat of the dryer and breakage of hair

Unless you are using a two-in-one shampoo plus conditioner, spend the extra two minutes to condition your dog's coat after bathing. The benefits of doing so will be appreciated by both yourself and your dog that will have overall healthy skin and a coat with a natural shine.

Styptic Powder: you will always want to avoid causing any pain when trimming your Miniature Golden Retriever's toenails, because you don't want to destroy their trust in you regularly performing this necessary task.

However, accidents do happen, therefore if you accidentally cut into the vein in the toenail, know that you will cause your dog pain, and that the toenail will bleed. Therefore, it is always a good idea to keep some styptic powder (often called *"Kwik Stop")* in your grooming kit.

Dip a moistened finger into the powder and apply it, with pressure, to the end of the bleeding nail because this is quickest way to stop a nail from bleeding in just a few seconds.

TIP

If you do not have styptic powder available, there are several home remedies that can help stop the bleeding, including a mixture of baking soda and cornstarch, or simply cornstarch alone.

A cold, wet teabag or rubbing with scent-free soap can also be effective. These home remedies will not be as instantly effective as styptic powder.

Ear Powders: which can be purchased at any pet store, are designed to help keep your dog's ears dry while at the same time inhibiting the growth of bacteria that can lead to infections. Ear powders are also used when removing excess hair growth from inside a dog's ear canal as the powder makes it easier to grip the hair.

Ear Cleaning Solutions: your local pet store will offer a wide variety of ear cleaning creams, drops, oils, rinses or wipes specially formulated for cleaning your dog's ears. As well, there are also many home remedies that will just as efficiently clean your dog's ears without the high price tag.

NOTE: because a dog's ears are a very sensitive area, always read the

labels before purchasing products and avoid any solutions that list alcohol as the main ingredient.
Home Ear Cleaning Solutions: the following are three effective home solutions that will efficiently clean your dog's ears:

Witch Hazel is a natural anti-inflammatory that works well to cleanse and protect against infection while encouraging faster healing of minor skin traumas.

A 50:50 solution of **Organic Apple Cider Vinegar and Purified Water** has been used as an external folk medicine for decades. This mixture is a gentle and effective solution that kills germs while naturally healing.

A 50:50 solution of **Hydrogen Peroxide and Purified Water** is useful for cleansing wounds and dissolving earwax.

Whatever product you decide to use for cleaning your dog's ears, always be careful about what you put into your dog's ears and thoroughly dry them after cleaning.

Canine Toothpastes: when it comes time to brush a dog's teeth, this is where many guardians fail miserably, often using the excuse that *"my dog doesn't like it"*. Whether they like it or otherwise is not the issue, because in order to keep your dog healthy, they <u>must</u> have healthy teeth and the only way to ensure this, is to brush their teeth every day.

The many canine toothpastes on the market are usually flavored with beef or chicken in an attempt to appeal to the dog's taste buds, while others may be infused with mint or some other breath-freshening ingredient in an attempt to appeal to humans by improving the dog's breath.

Honestly, your dog is not going to be begging for you to brush his or her teeth no matter how tasty the paste might be, therefore, effectiveness in the shortest period of time will be more of a deciding factor than whether or not your dog prefers the taste of the toothpaste.

Some dog toothpastes contain baking soda, which is the same mild abrasive found in many human pastes, and they are designed to gently scrub the teeth. However, just how much time you will have to spend scrubbing your dog's teeth before they've had enough may be too minimal to make these pastes very effective.
Other types of canine toothpastes are formulated with enzymes that are

designed to work chemically by breaking down tartar or plaque in the dog's mouth. These pastes do not need to be washed off your dog's teeth and are safe for them to swallow. Whether or not they remain on the dog's teeth long enough to do any good might be debatable.

TIP

Old-fashioned hydrogen peroxide cleans while killing germs and keeping teeth white. Just dip your dog's toothbrush in a capful of hydrogen peroxide, shake off the excess, and brush their teeth. There will be such a small amount in your dog's mouth that you don't need to worry about them swallowing it.

Paw Creams: depending upon activity levels and the types of surfaces our canine counterparts usually walk on, they may suffer from cracked or rough pads. You can restore resiliency and keep your Miniature Golden Retriever's paws in healthy condition by regularly applying a cream or lotion to protect their paw pads and a good time to do this is just after you have clipped their nails.

NOTE: if you live in a hot climate, be aware that sidewalks, road surfaces and sandy beaches can get extremely hot for your dog's feet.

A dog is much closer to the hot surface, which means that on a hot day they will be feeling the effects of being heated from both the top and the bottom. If you live in a very hot climate, choose to walk them during the cooler hours of the day, or walk them on grassy or shaded areas only.

Organic Pest Control: CedarCide is a company that makes 100% safe, organic products to control biting bugs on your furry friends without worrying about harmful chemicals that are not good for you, your children or your canine companions.

Simply spray it on and bugs of any sort that come into contact with the solution will be dead, while your dog's coat will be shiny and fresh smelling, like the inside of a cedar chest.

11. Professional Grooming

If you decide that you are not interested in bathing or grooming your retriever yourself, you will want to locate a trusted professional service to do this for you. The best way to find a groomer is to ask others who they use and whether they are happy with the results.

An average price for professionally bathing and grooming a Miniature Golden Retriever will usually start around \$40 (£24.75) and could be considerably more depending upon the size of the dog and whether the salon is also trimming nails or expressing anal glands.

Chapter 13: Socializing

Most Miniature Goldens have a naturally friendly temperament and when properly and continually socialized, will be friendly and happy to greet other dogs and people.

However, this does not mean that you can be lax about exposing them to different people, animals, places and unfamiliar sights and sounds when they are puppies, because this is a very important part of their young education and you want them to grow up to be a friendly and confident adult.

Much of how any dog behaves will depend entirely upon you, how extensively they were socialized as a puppy and how much they are continually being socialized throughout their life because without proper socialization, even the most naturally friendly dog can become neurotic, unsociable and learn to act out aggressively toward unknown dogs or people.

Never make the mistake of thinking that you only need to socialize a young puppy and then they will be fine for the rest of their life, as all dogs require constant socializing and once they reach adolescence, their personality can really begin to assert itself.

All dogs need to be exposed to different people, dogs, places and unusual sights and sounds when they are puppies and throughout their adult life.

Any dog that is not regularly socialized may become shy or suspicious of unfamiliar or unusual people or circumstances, which could lead to nervous or fearful behavior, which can then lead to aggression.

1. With Other Dogs and Pets

Generally speaking, the majority of an adult dog's habits and behavioral traits will be formed between the ages of birth and one year of age.

This is why it will be very important to introduce your Mini Golden puppy to a wide variety of locations, sights, sounds, smells and situations during the most formative period in their young life, which is usually the first 16 weeks.

Your puppy will learn how to behave in all these various circumstances by following your lead, feeling your energy and watching how you react in every situation.

For instance, never accidentally reward your puppy or dog for displaying nervousness, fear or growling at another dog or person by picking them up.

Picking up a puppy or dog at a time when they are displaying unbalanced energy actually turns out to be a reward for them, and you will be teaching them to continue with this type of behavior.

Picking up a puppy places them in a top dog position, where they have the higher ground and literally (because they are higher up) become more dominant than the person or dog they may have just growled at.

The correct action to take in such a situation is to gently correct your puppy with a firm yet calm energy by distracting them with a "no", or a quick sideways snap of the leash to get their attention back on you, so that they learn to let you deal with the situation on their behalf.

If you allow a fearful, nervous or shy puppy deal with situations that unnerve them without your direction, they may learn to react with fear or aggression to unfamiliar circumstances and you will have created a problem that could escalate into something more serious as they grow older.

The same is true of situations where a young puppy may feel the need to protect itself from a larger or older dog that may come charging in for a sniff. It is the guardian's responsibility to protect the puppy so that they do not feel that they must react with fear or aggression in order to protect themselves.

Once your puppy has received all their vaccinations, you can take them out to public dog parks and various locations where many dogs and people are found.

Before allowing them to interact with other dogs or puppies, take them for a disciplined walk on leash so that they will be a little tired and less likely to immediately pounce excitedly on all other dogs.

Keep your puppy on leash and close beside you, because most young puppies are a bundle of out of control energy, and you need to protect them while teaching them how far they can go before they may get themselves into trouble with adult dogs that might not appreciate their excited playfulness.

Remember that they may not have experienced the company of other dogs since you brought them home, and now that they have completed their course of vaccinations, they will understandably be excited and perhaps a little hesitant about seeing dogs again.

Keep a close watch on your Miniature Golden Retriever puppy to make sure they are not being overwhelmed by too many other dogs, or getting overly excited and stressed or nervous, because it is your job to protect your puppy.

If your puppy shows any signs of aggression or domination toward another puppy, dog or person, you must immediately step in and calmly discipline them, otherwise by doing nothing you will be agreeing with their behavior and will be allowing them to get into situations that could become serious behavioral issues as they grow in age and size.

No matter the age or size of your puppy, allowing them to display aggression or domination over another dog or person is never a laughing matter and this type of behavior must be immediately curtailed.

2. With Other People

Take your puppy everywhere with you and introduce them to many different people of all ages, sizes and ethnicities so they will learn what is normal. This will be easy to do, because most people will automatically be drawn to you when they see you have a puppy.

Most humans will want to interact with your puppy and if they ask to hold your puppy this is a good opportunity to socialize your puppy and show them that humans are friendly.

Do not let others (especially young children) play roughly with your puppy or squeal at them in a high-pitched voices because this can be very frightening for a young puppy. You do not want to teach your puppy that humans are a source of crazy, excited energy.

Be especially careful when introducing your puppy to young children who may accidentally hurt your puppy, because you don't want your dog to become fearful of children as this could lead to aggression issues later on in life.

Explain to children that your puppy is very young and that they must be calm and gentle when playing or interacting in any way.

3. Within Different Environments

It can be a big mistake not to take the time to introduce your Miniature Golden Retriever puppy to a wide variety of different environments because when they are not comfortable with different sights and sounds, this could cause them possible trauma later in their adult life.

Be creative and take your puppy everywhere you can imagine when they are young so that no matter where they travel, whether strolling along a noisy city sidewalk or beside a peaceful shoreline, they will be equally comfortable.

Do not make the mistake of only taking your puppy into areas where you live and will always travel because they need to also be comfortable visiting areas you might not often visit, such as noisy construction sites, airports or a shopping area across town.

Your puppy needs to see all sorts of sights, sounds and situations so that they will not become fearful should they need to travel with you to any of these areas.

Your puppy will take their cues from you, which means that when you are calm and in control of every situation, they will learn to be the same because they will trust your lead.

For instance, take them to the airport where they can watch people and hear planes landing and taking off or take them to a local park where they can see a baseball game, or for a stroll beside a schoolyard at recess time when noisy children are out playing, or take them to the local zoo or farm and let them get a close up look at horses, pigs and ducks.

Again, never think that socialization is something that only takes place when your dog is a young puppy, as proper socialization is ongoing for your dog's entire life.

4. Loud Noises

Many dogs can show extreme fear of loud noises, such as fireworks or thunderstorms.

When you take the time to desensitize your Miniature Golden Retriever to these types of noises when they are very young, it will be much easier on them during stormy weather or holidays such as Halloween or New Year's when fireworks are often a part of the festivities.

You can purchase CD's that are a collection of unusual sounds, such as vacuums or hoovers, airplanes, sirens, smoke alarms, fireworks, people clapping hands, screaming children, and more (or you can easily make your own), that you can play while working in your kitchen or relaxing in your living room or lounge.

When you play these sounds and pretend that everything is normal, the next time your puppy or dog hears these types of sounds elsewhere, they will not become upset or agitated because they have learned to ignore them.

TIP

BUBBLE wrap is also another simple way to desensitize a dog that is fearful of popping sounds. Show them the bubble wrap, pop a few of the cells and if they do not run away, give them a treat. You can start with the bubble wrap that has small, quieter cells, and then graduate them to the larger celled (louder) bubble wrap.

Also make sure that you get your young puppy used to the sounds of thunder and fireworks at an early age because these types of shrieking, crashing, banging and popping sounds of fireworks or thunder as well as the high pitched beeping of household smoke and fire alarms can be so traumatic and unsettling for many dogs, that sometimes, no matter how much you try to calm your dog or pretend that everything is fine, there is little you can do.

Some dogs literally lose their minds when they hear the loud popping or screeching noises of fireworks and alarms and start trembling, running or trying to hide and you cannot communicate with them at all.

Make sure that your dog cannot harm itself trying to escape from these types of noises, and if possible, hold them until they begin to relax.
If your dog loses it's mind when it hears these types of noises, simply avoid taking them anywhere near fireworks and if at times when they

might hear these noises going off outside, play your inside music or TV louder than you might normally, to help disguise the exterior noise of fireworks or thunder.

Some dogs will respond well to wearing a *"ThunderShirt",* which is specifically designed to alleviate anxiety or trauma associated with loud rumbling, popping or banging noises.

The idea behind the design of the ThunderShirt is that the gentle pressure it creates is similar to a hug that, for some dogs, has a calming effect.

Do not underestimate the importance of taking the time to continually (not just when they are puppies) socialize and desensitize your puppy to all manner of sights, sounds, individuals and locations because to do so will be teaching them to be a calm and well balanced member of your family that will quietly follow you in every situation.

Chapter 14: Training

1. Trainability

While the loyal and affectionate Miniature Golden Retriever has been designed to be a companion dog, their DNA is strongly based in the hunting dog world and they will still be a highly intelligent and active dog that requires rules and boundaries that includes daily physical and mental stimulation.

What the dog thinks: "Just teach me – I can do anything!"

The eager to learn and easy to train Miniature Golden Retriever is very intelligent and you could teach this dog to do just about anything. This is a dog that will live for pleasing you and will excel at Advanced Obedience and any number of canine sports.

Exercise and ongoing training is especially important for highly intelligent and active dogs, and the Mini Golden will need fair, firm guidance and discipline from a young age, which includes rules and boundaries so that the dog firmly grasps that you are the boss and the awareness of the line they cannot ever cross.

You will need to exercise your Mini for a minimum of 30 minutes to an hour at least twice a day, with plenty of opportunity for them to run freely with other dogs or play games. This is a dog that required a lot of your time and attention and their ongoing education should be a daily occurrence.

Before you invest the considerable funds toward purchasing a Miniature Golden Retriever, make absolutely certain that you have the considerable time and energy to devote to their exercise and training.

The Miniature Golden Retriever is a very intelligent dog that loves to learn, so long as it's not boring. This dog needs plenty of praise and rewards and positive incentive during training and you will want to start training basic commands as soon as you bring him or her home (8 – 10 weeks).

Even at the young age of 8 weeks, this very smart puppy is highly capable of learning anything you can teach and if you wait until they are six months old before beginning any serious training program you could already have a headstrong problem on your hands and a young dog that is unwilling to heed your commands.

Keep in mind that dogs (of any breed) who are not afforded the opportunity for daily walks and exercise appropriate to their energy level outside of their yard and home can be much more likely to develop behavioral problems. The backbone of helping to develop a well-balanced and happy dog is to provide them with a routine that provides them with the chance to play, sniff and search every day.

Stress shortens all lives, and if you allow your dog to have the leadership role and feel that he or she must guard and protect you from all other animals and people, you have just placed a heavy and stressful burden on the shoulders of a dog. Further, when they make the wrong decisions (such as acting out aggressively toward another dog or person), they can place themselves in a dangerous position that could cost them their life.

As a result of the Miniature Golden Retriever being a combination of three very intelligent and active breeds, they are alert and focused dogs with brilliant minds, which means that this breed usually will require a higher amount of mental stimulation and firm direction from their guardian, which involves plenty of supervision.

Higher mental stimulation means that the Mini Golden needs a guardian who can provide them with a disciplined daily routine involving tasks where they get to use their brain.

The Miniature Golden Retriever will excel at a wide variety of canine sports, such as Agility, Flyball, Frisbee, Dock Diving, Trick Training, Advanced Obedience and more.

As this highly intelligent and eager to please dog requires a moderate to high amount of daily exercise, if you have access to a bicycle, it may be a good idea to consider training them to a *"Springer Bicycle Jogger"* so they can receive a good amount of disciplined exercise in a short period of time.

The *"Springer Bicycle Jogger"* attachment for a bicycle is an ideal and safe way to adequately exercise this intelligent and energetic dog while still keeping them under leash control so that they cannot chase after a cat or other distraction.

The Springer easily attaches to any bicycle and the arm can be quickly removed when not needed. The large spring attaches to a harness on the dog and there is a quick release, break-away tab at the top of the rope in case the dog runs around one side of a pole while you and the bike are on the other side.

As well, the large spring in this arrangement ensures that if the dog tries to lunge or chase a squirrel that you and your bicycle remain stable. The Springer Bicycle Jogger attachment is a sturdy, well-made product that you can purchase online for approximately $130 (£89).

When training, remember that every dog is an opportunist, which means that any training sessions need to somehow benefit them so that they learn that performing certain tasks will reap them a reward or benefit that they want.

For instance, if your Mini Golden has developed an unwanted behavior, rather than by reacting to it, which is still the dog getting attention, even if it is negative attention, you must then teach him or her, in a positive way, what to do that does not involve them repeating the unwanted behavior.

What you can teach them depends entirely upon you and the time and patience you have to devote to their education, not on what some expert might tell you with respect to how smart this particular breed may or may not be. No matter what you decide to teach your dog, always train with patience and kindness and NEVER yell, hit or punish a dog during training, or at any time for that matter.

Using harsh, mean or loud training methods could frighten a Miniature Golden Retriever and cause them to shut down. As well, any sort of harsh treatment will cause your loyal dog to lose trust and respect for you as their leader, and depending on their particular personality, they could also learn to fear you, or to fight back, which is NOT the type of relationship you want to have with your dog.

All training sessions should be happy and fun-filled with plenty of food rewards and positive reinforcement, which will ensure that your dog is an attentive student who looks forward to learning new commands, tricks and routines.

2. Puppy Training Basics

Most humans believe that they need to take their young dog to puppy classes, and generally speaking, this is a good idea for any young Miniature Golden Retriever (after they have had all their vaccinations), because it will help to get them socialized.

Beyond puppy classes for socializations reasons, hiring a professional dog whisperer for personalized private sessions to train the humans may be far more valuable than training situations where there are multiple dogs and humans together in one class as this can be very distracting for everyone concerned.

a) Choosing a Discipline Sound

Choosing a *"discipline sound"* that will be the same for every human family member will make it much easier for your puppy to learn what they can or cannot do and will be very useful when warning your puppy before they engage in unwanted behavior.

The best types of sounds are short and sharp so that you and your family members can quickly say them and so that the sound will immediately get the attention of your puppy because you want to be able to easily interrupt them when they are about to make a mistake.

It doesn't really matter what the sound is, so long as it gets your dog's attention and everyone in the family is consistent.
A sound that is very effective for most puppies and dogs is a simple ***"UH"*** sound said sharply and with emphasis.

Most puppies and dogs respond immediately to this sound and if caught in the middle of doing something they are not supposed to be doing will quickly stop and give you their attention or back away from what they were doing.

b) Three Most Important Words

"Come", **"Sit"** and **"Stay"** will be the three most important words you will ever teach your puppy.

These three basic commands will ensure that your puppy remains safe in

almost every circumstance.
For instance, when your puppy correctly learns the "Come" command, you can always quickly bring them back to your side if you should see danger be approaching.

When you teach your puppy the "Sit" and "Stay" commands you will be further establishing your leadership role. A puppy that understands that their human guardian is their leader will be a safe and happy follower.

All that's necessary for effectively teaching your puppy their basic first commands is a calm, consistent approach, combined with your endless patience.

Many puppies are ready to begin training at about 10 to 12 weeks of age, however, be careful not to overdo it when they are less than four to six months of age, as their attention span will be short. Make your training sessions no more than 5 or 10 minutes, positive and pleasant with lots of praise and/or treats so that your puppy will be looking forward to their next session.

COME: while the intelligent Miniature Golden Retriever puppy will be capable of learning commands and tricks at a young age, the first and most important command you need to teach your puppy is the recall, or *"Come"* command.

Begin the "Come" command inside your home. Go into a larger room, such as your living room area. Place your puppy in front of you and attach their leash or a longer line to their Martingale collar, while you back away from them a few feet.

Say the command "Come" in an excited, happy voice and hold your arms open wide. If they do not immediately come to you, gently give a tug on the leash so that they understand that they are supposed to move toward you. When they come to you praise them and give a treat they really enjoy.

Once your puppy can accomplish a "Come" command almost every time inside your home, you can then graduate them to a nearby park or quiet outside area where you will repeat the process.

You may want to purchase an extra long, lightweight line (25 or 50 feet) so that you are always attached to your puppy and can encourage them in the right direction should they become distracted.

SIT: the "Sit" and "Stay" commands are both easy commands to teach that will help to keep your puppy safe and out of danger in almost every circumstance.

Find a quiet time to teach these commands when your puppy is not overly tired.

Ask your puppy to "Sit" and if they do not yet understand the command, show them what you mean by gently squeezing with your thumb and middle finger the area across the back that joins with their back legs. Do not just push them down into a sit as this can cause damage to their back or joints. When they sit, give them a treat and praise them.

When you say the word "Sit", at the same time show them the hand signal for this command. While you can use any hand signal, the universal hand signal for "Sit" is:

Right arm (palm open facing upward) parallel to the floor, and then raising your arm, while bent at the elbow toward your right shoulder.

Once your Miniature Golden Retriever is sitting reliably for you, remove the verbal "Sit" and replace it with the hand signal.

It's important to begin teaching hand signals during the adolescent stage of your puppy's life, because this will also help them to be more attentive and communicate in a way that is more natural for a dog — by watching you and feeling your energy, rather than always having to hear you speak a command.

Every time you take your Miniature Golden Retriever out for a walk, which is often a cause of excitement, get into the habit of asking them to sit quietly and patiently while you put on their leash — then ask them to sit and calmly wait while you put on your shoes or jacket.

After you approach the door, ask them to sit again while you open the door — again after you are on the other side of the door — ask them to sit while you lock the door. When you are methodical and deliberate and take your time with this, your dog will be able to connect the dots and will soon learn the new routine of being patient and paying attention to you.

If there are stairs or landings involved, ask them to sit at the top and also again at the bottom.

Every time you arrive at street intersection or a crosswalk, ask your puppy to sit again, and do this in reverse when coming back home. Also, every time you stop during your walk to speak to a neighbor, greet a friend or admire the view, ask your puppy to sit.

Every time you ask your young dog to sit for you, they are learning several things all at once — that they must remain calm while paying attention to you, that you are the boss and that they must look to you for direction and respect you as their leader.

Also, a sitting puppy is much more easy to control than one standing at the alert, ready to bolt out the door or jump on someone. As well, because the action of sitting helps to calm the mind of an excited puppy (or dog), teaching your puppy the "Sit" command is a very important part of their daily interactions with your family members as well as people you may meet when out on a walk.

When you ask your puppy to "Sit" before you interact in any way with them, before you go out or in every door, before you feed them, etc., you are helping to quiet their mind, while teaching them to look to you for direction, and at the same time making it more difficult for them to jump, lunge or disappear out a door.

STAY: once your puppy can reliably "Sit", say the word "Stay" and hold your outstretched arm, palm open toward their head and back away a few steps. If they try to follow, calmly say "No" and put them back into "Sit". Give a treat and then say again, "Stay" with the hand signal and back away a few steps.

Once your puppy is sitting and staying, you can then ask them to "Come". Don't forget to use the open arms hand signal for "Come." Be a little excited with the "Come" command so that your puppy will always enjoy correctly responding and immediately returning to you.

Practice these three basic commands everywhere you go, and use the "Sit" command as much as you can to ensure its success rate.

As your puppy gets older, and their attention span increases, you will be able to train for longer periods of time.

The hand signal for "stay" is: right arm fully extended toward your dog's head, palm open, hand bent up at the wrist.

TIP

IF YOU are right-handed, use your right arm and hand for the signal, and if you are left-handed, use your left arm and hand for the signal. Using your dominant hand will be much more effective because your strongest energy emanates from the palm of your dominant hand.

3. Beginner Leash Lesson

Equipment you will need: 4 or 6-foot leash and a Martingale training collar.

The most important ongoing bonding exercise you will experience with your new puppy is when you go out for your daily walks together.

Far, far too many people ignore this critical, multi-tasking time that is not only important for your puppy's exercise, it fulfills a multitude of their needs, including:

- Exercising their body
- Fulfilling their natural roaming urges
- Teaching them discipline, which engages their mind
- Learning to follow, trust and respect you
- Reinforcing that you are their leader

As soon as you bring your new puppy home you will want to teach them how to walk at your side while on leash without pulling.

Every time your puppy needs to go out to relieve his or herself, slip on their collar and snap on that leash.

At first your puppy may struggle or fight against having a collar around their neck, because the sensation will be new to them. However, at the same time they will want to go with you, so exercise patience and encourage them to walk with you.

Be careful never to drag them, and if they pull backwards and refuse to walk forward with you, simply stop for a moment, while keeping slight forward tension on the leash, until your puppy gives up and moves forward. Immediately reward them with your happy praise, and if they have a favorite treat, this can be an added incentive when teaching them to walk on their leash.

Always walk your puppy on your left side with the leash slack so that they learn that walking with you is a relaxing experience. Keep the leash short enough so that they do not have enough slack to get in front of you.

If they begin to create tension in the leash by pulling forward or to the side, simply stop moving, get them back beside you, and start over.

Be patient and consistent with your puppy and very soon they will understand exactly where their walking position is and will walk easily beside you without any pulling or leash tension.

Remember that walking with a new puppy is an exciting experience for them as they will want to sniff everything and explore their new world, so give them lots of understanding and don't expect them to be perfect all the time.

When your puppy is very young, and wanting to put everything in their mouths, walk them in a harness AND collar and leash, so that you can have a second leash attached to the harness.

All puppies want to put everything in their mouths, therefore, when they are wearing a collar and leash, AND a harness and leash, you will be able to easily lift them over cigarette butts or other garbage you may encounter while out walking.

Once they grow out of the habit of tasting all manner of garbage, you can dispense with the harness and second leash.

4. Surviving Adolescence

The adolescent period in a young Miniature Golden Retriever's life, between the ages of 6 and 12 months, is the transitional stage of both physical and psychological development when they are physically almost full grown in size, yet their minds are still developing and they are testing their boundaries and the limits that their human counterparts will endure.

This can be a dangerous time in a puppy's life because this is when they start to make decisions on their own and if they do not receive the leadership they need from their human guardians, can lead to the development of unwanted behaviors.

Learning how to make decisions on their own would be perfectly normal and desirable if your puppy were living in the wild, amongst a pack of dogs, because learning to make decisions would be necessary for their survival.

However, when living within a human environment, your puppy must always adhere to human rules and it will be up to their human guardians to continue their vigilant, watchful guidance in order to make sure that they do.

Many humans are lulled into a false sense of security when their new puppy reaches the age of approximately six months, because the puppy has been well socialized, they have been to puppy classes and long since been house trained.

The real truth is that the serious work is only now beginning and people and their new puppy could be in for a time of testing that could seriously challenge the relationship and leave the humans wondering if they made the right decision to share their home with a dog.

If the human side of the relationship is not prepared for this transitional time in their young dog's life, their patience may be seriously tried, and the relationship of trust and respect that has been previously built can be damaged, and could take considerable time to repair.

While not all adolescent puppies will experience a noticeable adolescent period of craziness, because every puppy is different, most young dogs do commonly exhibit at least some of the usual adolescent behaviors, including reverting to previous puppy behaviors.

Some of these adolescent behaviors might include destructive chewing of objects they have previously shown no interest in, selective hearing or ignoring previously learned commands, displaying aggressive behavior, howling uncontrollably, jumping on everyone, barking at everything that moves, or reverting to relieving themselves in the house, even though they were house trained months ago.

Keeping your cool and recognizing these adolescent signs is the first step toward helping to make this transition period easier on your puppy and all family members.

The first step to take that can help keep raging hormones at bay is to spay or neuter your puppy just prior to the onset of adolescence, at around four or five months of age.

While spaying or neutering a puppy will not entirely eliminate the adolescent phase, it will certainly help and at the same time will spare your puppy the added strain of both the physical and emotional changes that occur during sexual maturity.

As well, some female puppies will become extremely aggressive toward other dogs during a heat, and non-neutered males may become territorially aggressive and pick fights with other males.

Once your puppy has been spayed or neutered, you will want to become more active with your young dog, both mentally and physically by providing them with continued and more complex disciplined exercises.

This can be accomplished by enrolling your adolescent Miniature Golden Retriever in a dog whispering session or more advanced training class, which will help them to continue their socialization skills while also developing their brain.

Even though it may be more difficult to train during this period, having the assistance of a professional and continuing the experience of ongoing socialization amongst other dogs of a similar size can be invaluable, as this is the time when many young dogs begin to show signs of antisocial behavior with other dogs as well as unknown humans.

When your Miniature Golden Retriever is provided with sufficient daily exercise and continued socialization with unfamiliar dogs, people and places that provide interest and expand their mind, they will be able to transition through the adolescent stage of their life much more seamlessly.

5. Releasing Energy

The adolescent period in any puppy's life is a time of boundless energy and you will need to find ways to safely allow them to release this energy every day.

Since most humans cannot walk nearly fast enough to accommodate the needs of an energetic puppy, you will first want to walk your Miniature Golden Retriever beside you on leash, and then find a safe place where they can run off leash, either chasing a ball, retrieving a Frisbee or playing and running in an enclosed area with other similar sized dogs where you can always supervise.

6. The Unruly Adolescent

If your puppy happens to be especially unruly during their adolescent phase, you will need to simply provide them with more outlets for safely exercising and releasing their energy while limiting their opportunities for making mistakes.

For instance, a puppy who is digging up the yard or chewing up just about anything they can get their teeth on will need to be closely supervised so that you can direct their energy into less harmful pursuits.

It does absolutely no good to yell at your puppy for engaging in behavior you are not happy with, and in fact, yelling or getting angry will only desensitize your young dog from listening to any of your commands.

Although you may eventually get the results you want, if you yell loud enough, your puppy will then be reacting out of fear, rather than respect, and this will be damaging to your relationship.

Displaying calm, yet assertive energy is the ONLY energy that works well to help your adolescent puppy understand what is required of them.

All other human emotions (frustration, anger, impatience, sadness, excitement) are “read” by puppies and dogs as being unstable, and not only will the Miniature Golden Retriever not understand these emotions, they will not respect you for displaying these types of unstable energies.

An extremely rambunctious adolescent Miniature Golden Retriever may need to have their free run of the house curtailed so that they are confined to areas where you can easily supervise them.

Make sure they are within eyesight at all times, so that if they do find an opportunity to make a mistake, you can quickly show them what is permitted and what is not.

Adolescence may also be a time when you might have to insist that your young companion sleeps in their crate with the door closed whenever you cannot supervise, as well as at bedtime so they continue to understand that

you have firm rules.
As well, keeping on top of house training is also a good idea during the adolescent period of your puppy's life because some adolescent puppies may become stubborn and forget that they are already house trained.

This means actually taking the time to be involved in the process by leashing up your pup and physically taking them outside whenever they need to relieve themselves.

Many times humans that have back yards tend not to be very involved in the housebreaking routine because they just open a door and let their dogs run free in the back yard.

Too many people with convenient yards simply do not participate at all in the bathroom routine of their young dogs and thereby miss out on endless opportunities to reinforce who is the boss.

7. Rewarding Unwanted Behavior

Often humans make the mistake of accidentally rewarding unwanted behavior.

It is very important to recognize that any attention paid to an overly excited, out of control, adolescent puppy, even negative attention, is likely going to be rewarding for your puppy.

Therefore, when you engage with an out of control puppy, you end up actually rewarding them, which will encourage them to continue more of this unwanted behavior.

Be aware that chasing after a puppy when they have taken something they are not supposed to have, picking them up when they are barking or showing aggression, pushing them off when they jump on you or other people, or yelling when they refuse to come when called, are all forms of attention that can actually be rewarding for most puppies.

As your dog's guardian, it will be your responsibility to provide calm and consistent structure for your puppy, which will include finding acceptable and safe ways to allow your puppy to vent their energy without being destructive or harmful to property, other dogs, humans, or the actual puppy.

Activities that create or encourage an overly excited puppy, such as rough games of tug-o-war, wild games of chase through the living room, or overly aggressive or excited play sessions with another dog or puppy, should be immediately curtailed, so that your adolescent puppy learns how to control their energy and play quietly and appropriately without jumping on everyone or engaging in barking or mouthy behavior.

Further, if your adolescent puppy displays excited energy simply from being petted by you, your family members or any visitors, you will need to teach yourself, your family and your friends to ignore your puppy until they calm down. Otherwise, you will be inadvertently teaching your puppy that the touch of humans means excitement.

For instance, when you continue to engage with an overly excited puppy or dog, you are rewarding them for out of control behavior and literally teaching them that when they see humans, you want them to display excited energy. Even worse, once your puppy has learned that humans are a source of excitement, you will then have to work very long and hard to reverse this behavior.

Children are often a source of excitement that can cause an adolescent puppy to be extremely wound up.

Do not allow your children to engage with an adolescent puppy unless you are there to supervise and teach the children appropriate and calm ways to interact with the puppy.

In order to keep everyone safe, it is very important that your Miniature Golden Retriever puppy learn at an early age that neither children nor adults are sources of excitement.

You can help develop the mind of an adolescent Mini Golden and the minds of growing children at the same time by teaching children that your puppy needs structured walks and by showing them how to play fetch, search, hide and seek, or how to teach the puppy simple tricks and obedience skills that will be fun and positive interaction for everyone.

8. Back to "Sit" Basics

When your puppy is going through what could be a belligerent and trying adolescence, when it seems that they have forgotten everything they may have already previously learned, this is an especially good time to revisit the simple "Sit" command.

Now, in order to help re-establish your leadership role, you will want to ask your puppy to sit at every opportunity because the simple act of "sitting" will help to calm an excited mind and will get your puppy's focus back on you.

Every time you take your dog out for a walk, which is often a cause of excitement, get into the habit of asking them to sit quietly and patiently while you put on their leash — then ask them to sit and calmly wait while you put on your shoes or jacket.

After you approach the door, ask them to sit again while you open the door — again after you are on the other side of the door — ask them to sit while you lock the door.

When you are methodical and deliberate and take your time with this, your dog will be able to connect the dots and will soon learn the new routine of being patient and paying attention to you.

If there are stairs or landings involved, ask them to sit at the top and also again at the bottom.

Every time you arrive at street intersection or a crosswalk, ask your puppy to sit again, and do this in reverse when coming back home. Also, every time you stop during your walk to speak to a neighbor, greet a friend or admire the view, ask your puppy to sit.

Every time you ask your young dog to sit for you, they are learning several things all at once — that they must remain calm while paying attention to you, that you are the boss and that they must look to you for direction and respect you as their leader. Also, a sitting puppy is much more easy to control than one standing at the alert, ready to bolt out the door or jump on someone.

Once your puppy is reliably sitting for you at least 50% of the time with voice command, also include the hand signal for "Sit", so that they will hear the word and also see the signal.

While you can use any hand signal, the universal hand signal for "Sit" is: Right arm (palm open facing upward) parallel to the floor, and then raising your arm, while bent at the elbow toward your right shoulder.

Once your dog is sitting reliable for you, remove the verbal “Sit” and replace it with the hand signal.

It’s important to begin teaching hand signals during the adolescent stage of your puppy’s life, because this will also help them to be more attentive and communicate in a way that is more natural for a dog — by watching you and feeling your energy, rather than always having to hear you speak a command.

As well, because the action of sitting helps to calm the mind of an excited puppy (or dog), teaching your puppy the “Sit” command is a very important part of their daily interactions with your family members as well as people you may meet when out on a walk.

When you ask your puppy to "Sit" before you interact in any way with them, before you go out or in every door, before you feed them, etc., you are helping to quiet their mind, while teaching them to look to you for direction, and at the same time making it more difficult for them to jump, lunge or disappear out a door.

The adolescent stage in a young dog’s life is the perfect time to begin teaching hand signals for all your common commands, because they must look at you to understand what is expected of them, and when they are looking at you, they are more focused and less likely to take matters into their own paws.

9. Giving Up is Not an Option

Too often we humans get frustrated and give up on our dogs when they change from being the cute, cuddly and mostly obedient little puppy they once were and become all kinds of trouble you never bargained for as they grow into their adolescent stage.

Often, it will be during the confusing adolescent stage of a dog’s life that they find themselves abandoned and behind bars as their humans who promised to love and protect them, leave their once loved fur friend at the local pound or SPCA.

First of all, not all dogs go through a crazy adolescent period, and secondly, even if they do, please read this section carefully, because you can live through puppy adolescence and come out the other side relatively unscathed and a much more knowledgeable and patient guardian.

Congratulations are in order because you've been successful with potty training your young puppy and with teaching them to sleep in their own kennel at night.

Further, you've lived through the teething troubles, the chewing and the hand nipping and you no longer have to get up at 3:00 a.m. to let your puppy out to go potty. As well, you've taught your puppy their first few basic commands, and socialized them with many other dogs, people and places, so you should feel proud of all your accomplishments and the leaps and bounds you and your puppy have accomplished together over the last several months.

Even though your adolescent puppy may be starting to act like a Tasmanian devil, and you may be having second thoughts, now is not the time to give up on them and yourself just because it may seem like someone switched your dog when you weren't looking.

Now is the time to remain calmly consistent and persistent, and to know that you will eventually be able to enjoy the happy rewards that all those months of diligent puppy training have brought to your relationship.

Yes, it can be quite a shock when what used to be your well behaved little darling who never chewed anything they weren't supposed to suddenly takes it into their head to eat all the tassels off your Persian rug or chew through a seat belt in your vehicle during the short 15 minutes you were buying dog food at your local pet store.

Even more disconcerting might be when your previously obedient and loving Miniature Golden Retriever puppy, who always listened to your directions, suddenly appears to have gone deaf and can't remember their name when you call them to follow you inside the house, and instead they take off running after a cat three blocks away.

And then, what happened to that quiet little puppy that never appeared to have a mean bone in their body that now spends most of their time at the window barking and growling at everything and everyone passing by?

Welcome to the world of canine adolescence where it appears that your puppy has turned into some sort of monster and all your previous hard work was for nothing. This is the time when your patience may be

seriously tested. Of course, this dramatic switch from being the world's best puppy into the monster you can no longer control is not true for all puppies, as every puppy is unique.
However, being prepared for the worst will help you ride any impending storm and get you both safely out the other side where you can enjoy an even closer relationship than you previously had.

The adolescent phase may be very subtle for your puppy or on the other hand, it may be so dramatic that you're starting to feel guilty every time you drive past the local SPCA or dog pound because thoughts of rehoming are running through your head.

If you are at the stage with your puppy that you are having great difficulties and wondering if you made the right decision to share your home with a dog, rest assured that puppy adolescence is a normal phase of their development, which can be managed, and which will definitely pass.

As well, if you are finding yourself totally overwhelmed, there are many professionals who can provide valuable assistance to help you through this stage of your puppy's development.

For most puppies, adolescence will begin between the ages of five and seven months and this is also the time that you need to be making an appointment at your veterinarian's office to have your puppy spayed or neutered.

Although neutering or spaying will not prevent undesirable adolescent behavior entirely, it can certainly reduce the intensity of it, as during this period there are hormonal changes occurring that will affect your puppy's behavior.

While it's usually hormones that are the major cause of behavioral changes in your adolescent puppy, there are also physical changes occurring at the same time that you may not be aware of. For instance, your puppy will be going through physical growth spurts which might be causing them some pain, as well as changes related to growth in their brain while your puppy's cerebral cortex becomes more involved in thinking for itself.

Usually, during this time of brain growth, a puppy will be trying to make choices for itself, and may or may not yet be capable of making the right choices. This is why their behavior can appear to be quite erratic.

During the early adolescent period of brain development in your Miniature Golden Retriever puppy, the signals sometimes get mixed up and rerouted, which can result in the perplexing responses you might notice, when for instance, you ask you puppy to sit and they stare dumbly at you, even though they learned this command months ago.

Don't worry because your previous training will return.

10. Re-visit Puppy Training Basics

All that's necessary for effectively teaching your puppy their basic first commands is a calm, consistent approach, combined with your endless patience.

Many puppies are ready to begin training at about 10 to 12 weeks of age, and some will be ready at 8 weeks, however, be careful not to overdo it when they are less than four months of age, as their attention span may be short.

Make your training sessions no more than 5 or 10 minutes, positive and pleasant with lots of praise and/or treats so that your puppy will be looking forward to their next session. Also, introduce the hand signals that go along with the verbal commands so that once they learn both, you can remove the verbal commands in favor of just hand signals.

Return to the Puppy Training Basics and go over the "Come", "Sit" and "Stay" commands and use them every day, in every opportunity to help your young dog progress through their unpredictable adolescent period.

Basic Hand Signals

Important: introduce the hand signals that go along with the verbal commands so that once they learn both, you can remove the verbal commands in favor of just hand signals. When your dog becomes older, his or her hearing might be affected and in this case, you will be able to communicate with your dog just with hand signals.

Hand signal training is by far the most useful and efficient training method for every dog, including the Miniature Golden Retriever. This is because all too often we inundate our canine companions with a great deal of chatter and noise that they really do not understand because English is not their first language.

Contrary to what some humans might think, the first language of a Miniature Golden Retriever, or any dog, is a combination of sensing energy and watching body language, which requires no spoken word or sound.

Therefore, when we humans take the time to teach our dog hand signals for all their basic commands, we are communicating with them at a level they instinctively understand, plus we are helping them to become a focused follower, as they must watch us to understand what is required of them.

a) COME HAND SIGNAL: you can kneel down for this command or stay standing. Open your arms wide like you are hugging a very large tree. This hand signal can be seen from a long distance.

When first teaching hand signals to your Miniature Golden Retriever, always show the hand signal for the command at the same time you say the word.

If they are totally ignoring the command, it will be time to incorporate a light lunge line, which is a very long leash to help you teach the "Come" command.

Simply attach a 20-foot line to their collar and let them sniff about in a large yard or at your neighborhood park, then at your leisure, firmly ask them to "Come" and show the hand signal. If they do not immediately come to you, give a firm tug with the lunge line, so that they understand what you are asking of them.

If they still do not "Come" toward you, simply reel them in until they are in front of you. Then let them wander about again, until you are again ready to ask them to "Come".

Repeat this process until your Miniature Golden Retriever responds correctly at least 80% of the time. You can also reinforce the command by giving a treat when they come back to you when asked. It is important to make sure that returning to you is always a fun, pleasant and rewarding experience for your dog or puppy. Always ask them to "Sit" when they return to you and then praise them enthusiastically.

NOTE: the "Come" command is *THE* most important command you will ever teach your dog, therefore, <u>never</u> ask them to come to you if you are angry or upset or to punish them in any way, because you want them to be solid with this command, and never fear coming when called.

b) SIT HAND SIGNAL: right arm (palm open facing upward) parallel to the floor, and then raise your arm, while bent at the elbow toward your shoulder.

Sit is a very simple, yet extremely valuable command for all puppies and dogs.

If your dog is not sitting on command, try holding a treat above and slightly behind their head, so that when they look up for it they may automatically sit in order to see the treat they want.

Slowly remove the treat as reward and replace the treat with a "life reward", such as a chest rub or a scratch behind the ears and your happy smile.

If your dog is not particularly treat motivated, lift up and slightly back on the leash when asking them to sit (stand in front of them), and if they still are having difficulties, reach down with your free hand, place it across your dog's back at the place where the back legs join the hip and gently squeeze.

Remember -- Do NOT simply push down on your dog's back to force their hind legs to collapse under them as this pressure could harm their spine or leg joints.

c) STAY HAND SIGNAL: right armed fully extended toward your dog's head, palm open, hand bent up at the wrist.

Once your Miniature Golden Retriever is in the "Sit" position, ask them to "Stay" with both the verbal cue and the hand signal.

TIP

IF YOU are right-handed, use your right arm and hand for the signal, and if you are left-handed, use your left arm and hand for the signal. Using your dominant hand will be much more effective because your strongest energy emanates from the palm of your dominant hand.

While your dog is sitting and staying, slowly back away from them. If they move from their position, calmly put them back into Sit and ask them to

"Stay" again, using both the verbal cue and the hand signal.

Continue to practice this until your dog understands that you want them to stay sitting and not move toward you. With all commands, when your dog is just learning, be patient and always reward them with a treat and your happy praise for a job well done.

12. Simple Tricks

When teaching your Mini Golden tricks, in order to give them extra incentive, find a treat that they really like and give the treat as a reward and to help solidify a good performance. This is a dog that will really excel at trick training and they will learn very quickly.

Most dogs will be extra attentive during training sessions when they know that they will be rewarded with their favorite treats. If your dog is less than six months old when you begin teaching them tricks, keep your training sessions short (no more than 5 or 10 minutes) and fun, and as they become adults, you can extend your sessions as they will be able to maintain their focus for longer periods of time.

a) Shake a Paw: who doesn't love a dog that knows how to shake a paw? This is one of the easiest tricks to teach your Miniature Golden Retriever.

TIP

MOST DOGS are naturally either right or left pawed. If you know which paw your dog favors, ask them to shake this paw.

Find a quiet place to practice, without noisy distractions or other pets, and stand or sit in front of your dog. Place them in the sitting position and have a treat in your left hand.

Say the command *"Shake"* while putting your right hand behind their left or right paw and pulling the paw gently toward yourself until you are holding their paw in your hand. Immediately praise them and give them the treat.

Most dogs will learn the "Shake" trick quite quickly, and very soon, once you put out your hand, your Miniature Golden Retriever will immediately lift their paw and put it into your hand, without your assistance or any verbal cue.

Practice every day until they are 100% reliable with this trick, and then it will be time to add another trick to their repertoire.

b) Roll Over: you will find that just as your Miniature Golden Retriever is naturally either right or left pawed, they will also naturally want to roll either to the right or the left side. Take advantage of this by asking your dog to roll to the side they naturally prefer.

Sit with your dog on the floor and put them in a lie down position. Hold a treat in your hand and place it close to their nose without allowing them to grab it, and while they are in the lying position, move the treat to the right or left side of their head so that they have to roll over to get to it.

You will very quickly see which side they want to naturally roll to, and once you see this, move the treat to this side. When they roll over to this side, immediately give them the treat and praise them.

You can say the verbal cue *"Over"* while you demonstrate the hand signal motion (moving your right hand in a circular motion) or moving the treat from one side of their head to the other with a half circle motion.

c) Sit Pretty: while this trick is a little more complicated, and most dogs pick up on it very quickly, remember that every dog is different so always exercise patience.

Find a quiet space with few distractions and sit or stand in front of your dog and ask them to "Sit".

Have a treat nearby (on a countertop or table) and when they sit, use both of your hands to lift up their front paws into the sitting pretty position, while saying the command *"Sit Pretty"*. Help them balance in this position while you praise them and give them the treat.

Once your Miniature Golden Retriever can do the balancing part of the trick quite easily without your help, sit or stand in front of your dog while asking them to *"Sit Pretty"* and hold the treat above their head, at the level their nose would be when they sit pretty.

TIP

WHEN FIRST beginning this trick, place your Miniature Golden Retriever beside a wall so they can use the wall to help them balance.

If they attempt to stand on their back legs to get the treat, you may be holding the treat too high, which will encourage them to stand on their back legs to reach it. Go back to the first step and put them back into the *"Sit"* position and again lift their paws while their backside remains on the floor.

Sit Pretty hand signal: hold your straight arm, fully extended, over your dog's head with a closed fist.

Make this a fun and entertaining time for both of you and practice a few times every day until they can *"Sit Pretty"* on hand signal command every time you ask.

A young puppy should be able to easily learn these basic tricks before they are six months old and when you are patient and make your training sessions short and fun for your dog, they will be eager to learn more.

13. Adult Training

The Miniature Golden Retriever is an exceptionally intelligent, athletic breed that will be skillful in many different sports and services, therefore, in order to ensure a happy and healthy companion, make sure that you get them involved in as much activity as possible, including advanced training and other canine sports.

When your dog is a full grown adult (approximately two years of age), you will definitely want to begin more complicated or advanced training sessions. They will be an attentive student and when you have the desire and patience, there is no end to the commands, tricks, routines or canine sports you can teach a willing Miniature Golden Retriever.

For instance, you may wish to teach your adult dog more advanced tricks, such as how to dance, or the opposite sided paw shakes or rollovers, which are more difficult than you might expect.

If you and your dog are really enjoying learning new tricks together, you might want to advance to teaching them the hand signals for "*commando crawl*", how to *"speak"* or to *"jump through the human hoop"*, or perhaps get them involved in a fun sport.

All of these tricks and many more are fun to teach and will exercise both your dog's mind and body by taking advantage of their natural ability to excel.

As well, the more control you have over your Miniature Golden Retriever, the easier it will be to teach them a fun sport, such as Agility or Rally and the only restriction to how far you can go with training your adult dog will be your imagination and their personal ability or desire to perform.

14. Behavioral Issues

It can be difficult, if not impossible to generalize or speculate with respect to alleviating possible behavioral issues or problems you may encounter with your dog because, in most cases, a dog suffering from behavioral issues requires the assistance of a dog whisperer or dog psychologist.

When reading anything about how to prevent or cure behavioral issues, please be aware that behavioral problems most often cannot be properly assessed or cured by reading a book.

The reason for this is because there are just too many variables and unique situations, individual dogs, individual humans, unique circumstances, and endless reasons why they may have developed any particular behavioral issue.

Therefore, without knowing the dog's particulars and all the history of what has transpired between the Miniature Golden and their guardian that came before or how the problem might have manifested itself, attempting to write about how to cure a particular issue will be no more than a best guess.

This is why someone whose dog is suffering from a specific behavioral issue that is in turn at the least embarrassing, or at the worst dangerous, and driving the humans and the entire neighborhood crazy, must be properly addressed by engaging the services of a competent, professional dog whisperer (psychologist or behaviorist) who can ask many questions, properly assess the situation and then design a unique plan for alleviating the problem.

15. Overheating

a) Outside: be very careful when training or walking your dog outside during hot weather, so that you do not allow them to become overheated.

When it's warm outside, always carry water with you to help keep them hydrated and do not expect them to exercise for as long as they might during cooler weather.

TIP

YOU CAN easily help to keep them cooler on hot, sunny days by having them wear a light-weight vest that will help to reflect the heat.

Remember that dogs are closer to heated pavement, road surfaces or sandy beaches, which means that on a hot, sunny day, they will literally be heated from both the bottom and the top. If the surface is very hot, do not allow them to walk on it. Instead, take them to a grassy or shaded area for their exercise.

b) Inside Vehicles: never leave your dog alone inside a vehicle on a warm day, even for a few minutes.

On a warm, summer's day that may seem a pleasant 72°F to us humans (22.2 Celsius), inside a metal vehicle the temperature can quickly climb to 120°F (48.8 Celsius), even with the windows left open, in a short ten minutes.

In many parts of the world it is a crime to leave a dog unattended inside a vehicle and you may return to find that your window has been broken and your dog rescued by local authorities that may have intervened, or much more serious and tragic, you may return to find that your dog has died from heat exhaustion.

As well, you might think that leaving the windows cracked and parking underneath a tree that is providing shade will be good enough for your dog. Think again, because dogs are not as efficient as humans when it comes down to regulating their body temperature and they could seriously suffer, or even die, while you're off shopping or enjoying your iced latte.

A good and smart rule of thumb that will keep you and your dog safe on warm days: <u>never</u> leave them alone in your vehicle.

NOTE: also never leave your dog alone in a vehicle during cold weather because they can just as quickly suffer from hypothermia because your vehicle will turn into a large refrigerator during cold winter days just as quickly as it can turn into a deadly oven during the summer heat.

Chapter 15: Poisonous Foods & Plants

1. Poisonous Foods

While some dogs are smart enough not to want to eat foods that can harm or kill them, there are those canine companions that will eat absolutely anything they can get their teeth on, whether or not it's food.

If your dog is highly food motivated, in order to keep them safe and healthy, it will be very important to keep cupboards containing any food or poisonous products tightly closed and out of their reach. This will also include any area where you might store garbage because if they can smell it, they will figure out how to get to it. As conscientious guardians for our furry friends, it will always be our responsibility to make certain that when we share our homes with a dog, we never leave foods (or other products) that could be toxic or lethal to them easily within their reach.

While there are many foods that can be toxic to a dog, the following alphabetical list contains some of the more common foods that can seriously harm or even kill our dogs including:

Bread Dough: if your dog eats bread dough, their body heat will cause the dough to rise inside the stomach. As the dough expands during the rising process, alcohol is produced. Dogs who have eaten bread dough may experience stomach bloating, abdominal pain, vomiting, disorientation and depression. Because bread dough can rise to many times its original size, eating only a small amount will cause a problem for any dog.

Broccoli: the toxic ingredient in broccoli is isothiocynate. While it may cause stomach upset, it probably won't be very harmful unless the amount eaten is more than 10% of the dog's total daily diet.

Chocolate: contains theobromine, a chemical that is toxic to dogs in large enough quantities. Chocolate also contains caffeine, which is found in coffee, tea, and certain soft drinks. Different types of chocolate contain different amounts of theobromine and caffeine. For example, dark chocolate and baking chocolate or cocoa powder contain more of these compounds than milk chocolate does, therefore, a dog would need to eat more milk chocolate in order to become ill.

However, even a few ounces of chocolate can be enough to cause illness or death in a puppy or smaller dog, therefore, no amount or type of chocolate should be considered safe for a dog to eat. A dog suffering from having eaten chocolate may display symptoms that include diarrhea, vomiting, increased heart rate, restless behavior, muscle tremors, or seizures. If they have eaten enough of it, they could die within 24 hours of eating.

During many holidays such as Christmas, New Year's, Valentine's, Easter and Halloween, chocolate is often more easily accessible to curious dogs, especially from children who are not so careful with where they might keep their Halloween or Easter egg stash and who are an easy mark for a hungry dog.

In some cases, people unwittingly poison their dogs by offering them chocolate as a treat or leaving chocolate cookies or frosted cake easily within licking distance.

Caffeine: beverages containing caffeine, such as soda, tea, coffee, and chocolate, act as a stimulant and can accelerate your dog's heartbeat to a dangerous level. Dogs ingesting caffeine have been known to have seizures, some of which are fatal.

Cooked Bones: can be extremely hazardous for a dog because the bones become brittle when cooked which causes them to splinter when the dog chews on them. The splinters have sharp edges that have been known to become stuck in the teeth, and cause choking when caught in the throat or create a rupture or puncture of the stomach lining or intestinal tract.

Especially dangerous are cooked turkey and chicken legs, ham, pork chop and veal bones. Symptoms of choking include:

- Pale or blue gums
- Gasping breathing or panting
- Pawing or scratching at the face
- Slowed, shallow breathing
- Collapse and unconsciousness with dilated pupils

Grapes and Raisins: can cause acute (sudden) kidney failure in dogs. While it is not known what the toxic agent is in this fruit, clinical signs can occur within 24 hours of eating and include vomiting, diarrhea, and lethargy (tiredness).

Other signs of illness caused from eating grapes or raisins relate to the eventual shutdown of kidney functioning.

Garlic and Onions: contain chemicals that damage red blood cells by rupturing them so that they lose their ability to carry oxygen effectively, which leave the dog short of oxygen, causing what is called *"hemolytic anemia"*.

Poisoning can occur when a dog eats a large amount of garlic or onions all at once, or when eating repeated meals containing smaller amounts and cooking does not reduce the potential toxicity of onions and garlic.

NOTE: fresh, cooked, and/or powdered garlic or onions are commonly found in baby food, which is sometimes given to dogs when they are sick, therefore, be certain to carefully read food labels before feeding to your Miniature Golden Retriever.

Macadamia Nuts: are commonly found in candies and chocolates. Although the mechanism of macadamia nut toxicity is not well understood, the clinical signs in dogs having eaten these nuts include depression, weakness, vomiting, tremors, joint pain, and pale gums.

Signs can occur within 12 hours after eating. In some cases, symptoms can resolve themselves without treatment within 24 to 48 hours. However, keeping a close eye on your dog will be strongly recommended.

Mushrooms: mushroom poisoning can be fatal if certain species of mushrooms are eaten.

The most commonly reported severely toxic species of mushroom in the US is Amanita phalloides (Death Cap mushroom), which is also quite a common species found in most parts of Britain. Other Amanita species are also toxic.

This deadly mushroom is often found growing in grassy or wooded areas near various deciduous and coniferous trees, which mean that if you're out walking with your dog in the woods, they could easily find these mushrooms.
Eating them can cause severe liver disease and neurological disorders. If you suspect your dog has eaten these mushrooms, immediately take them to your veterinarian, as the recommended treatment is to induce vomiting and to give activated charcoal. Further treatment for liver disease may also be necessary.

Pits and Seeds: many seeds and pits found in a variety of fruits, including apples, apricots, cherries, pears and plums, contain cyanogenic glycosides that can cause cyanide poisoning in your dog. The symptoms of cyanide poisoning usually occur within 15-20 minutes to a few hours after eating and symptoms can include initial excitement, followed by rapid respiration rate, salivation or drooling, voiding of urine and feces, vomiting, muscle spasm, staggering, and coma before death.

Dogs suffering from cyanide poisoning that live more than 2 hours after onset of symptoms will usually recover.

Raw Salmon or Trout: Salmon Poisoning Disease (SPD) can be a problem for anyone who goes fishing with their dog, or feeds their dog a raw meat diet that includes raw salmon or trout.

When a snail is infected and then is eaten by the fish as part of the food chain, the dog is exposed when it eats the infected fish. A sudden onset of symptoms can occur 5-7 days after eating the infected fish. In the acute stages, gastrointestinal symptoms are quite similar to canine parvovirus.

SPD has a mortality rate of up to 90%, can be diagnosed with a fecal sample and is treatable if caught in time.

Prevention is simple, cook all fish before feeding it to your Miniature Golden Retriever and immediately see your veterinarian if you suspect that your dog has eaten raw salmon or trout.

Tobacco: all forms of tobacco, including patches, nicotine gum and chewing tobacco can be fatal to dogs if eaten. Signs of poisoning can appear quite rapidly (within an hour or less) and may include diarrhea, vomiting, a heightened state of activity, excessive drooling and panting.

Depending upon how much a dog may have eaten, more acute signs of poisoning may cause twitching, leading to collapse and coma due to heart attack that will cause death.

Never leave tobacco products within reach of your puppy or dog, and be careful not to let them pick up discarded cigarette butts when they are young puppies. If you suspect your dog has eaten cigarette butts, seek immediate veterinary help.

TIP

WHEN YOUR dog is a very young puppy, use a double leash, collar and harness arrangement, so that you can still teach them to walk on leash with a Martingale collar around their neck, but can also attach the second leash to their harness so that you can easily lift them over enticing cigarette butts or other toxic garbage they may be trying to eat during your walks.

Tomatoes: tomatoes contain a substance called atropine, which can cause tremors, dilated pupils and an irregular heartbeat in a puppy or dog that eats them. The greatest amount of atropine will be found in the stalks and leaves of the tomato plant, next is the green tomato (before it ripens), and then ripe tomatoes.

Xylitol: is an artificial sweetener often found in many candies, gums, breath mints, toothpastes and mouthwashes that is recognized by the National Animal Poison Control Center to be a poison risk to dogs.

When puppies or dogs eat products containing Xylitol, it causes a sudden release of insulin, which in turn causes low blood sugar, which can also cause liver damage.

Within 30 minutes after eating a product containing Xylitol, the dog may vomit, be lethargic (tired), and/or be uncoordinated. However, some signs of toxicity can also be delayed for hours or even for a few days. Xylitol toxicity in dogs can be fatal if left untreated.

Please be aware that the above list is just some of the more common foods that can be toxic or fatal to our furry friends and that there are many other foods we should never be feeding our dogs.

If you have one of those dogs who will happily eat anything that looks or smells even slightly like food, or even if not food, but is enticing for a puppy or dog to eat, be certain to keep these foods or products far away from your beloved Miniature Golden Retriever and you'll help them to live a long and healthy life.

2. Poisonous Household Plants

Many common house plants are actually poisonous to our canine companions, and although many dogs simply will ignore house plants, some will attempt to eat anything, especially puppies who want to taste everything in their new world.

More than 700 plant species contain toxins that may harm or be fatal to puppies or dogs, depending on the size of the puppy or dog and how much they may eat. Therefore, it is especially important to be aware of household plants that could be toxic when you are sharing your home with a new puppy.

Following is a short list of the more common household plants, what they look like, the different names they are known by, and what symptoms might be apparent if your puppy or dog decides to eat them.

Aloe Plant: also known as *"medicine plant or Barbados aloe",* is a very common succulent plant that is toxic to dogs. The toxic agent in this plant is Aloin. This bitter yellow substance is found in most aloe species and may cause vomiting and/or reddish urine.

Asparagus Fern: is also known as *"lace fern, emerald fern, emerald feather, sprengeri fern and plumosa fern"*. The toxic agent in this plant is sapogenin, which is a steroid found in a variety of plants. Repeated exposure to the berries of this plant cause vomiting, diarrhea and/or abdominal pain or skin inflammation.

Corn Plant: also known as *"ribbon plant, cornstalk plant, dragon tree*

and dracaena", is toxic to dogs. Saponin is the offensive chemical compound found in this plant. If the plant is eaten, vomiting (with or without blood), loss of appetite, depression and/or increased drooling can occur.

Cyclamen: also known as *"Sowbread",* is a pretty, flowering plant that, if eaten, can cause diarrhea, vomiting and increased salivation. If a dog eats a large amount of the plant's tubers, usually found underneath the soil at the root level, heart rhythm problems can occur, which may result in seizures or even death.

Dieffenbachia: also known as *"exotica, dumb cane and tropic snow"* contains a chemical that is a poisonous deterrent to animals. If a dog eats the plant, they will experience mouth irritation, especially on the tongue and lips that can lead to increased drooling, problems swallowing and vomiting.

Elephant Ear: also known as *"cape, caladium, malanga, pai, taro and via sori,"* contains a chemical which is similar to a chemical also found in dieffenbachia. A dog's toxic reaction to elephant ear is similar, including oral irritation, problems swallowing, increased drooling, and vomiting.

Heartleaf Philodendron: also known as "cordatum, split-leaf philodendron, fiddle leaf, fruit salad plant, horsehead philodendron, panda plant, red emerald, red princess, and saddle leaf", is a very common, easy-to-grow houseplant that contains a chemical irritating to the mouth, tongue and lips of dogs. An affected dog may also experience difficulty swallowing, vomiting and increased drooling.

Jade Plant: has many other names, including "baby jade, Chinese rubber plant, dwarf rubber plant, friendship tree, jade tree, or Japanese rubber plant". While exactly what is toxic to dogs in this plant is unknown, a dog eating a Jade plant can suffer from loss of coordination and depression as well as a slowed heart rate.

Lilies: some plants of the lily family can be toxic to dogs. The peace lily (also known as Mauna Loa) is known to be toxic to dogs. Eating the peace lily or calla lily can cause vomiting, irritation to the dog's tongue and lips, problems swallowing and increased drooling.

Satin Pothos: (silk pothos), if eaten by a dog, the plant may cause irritation to the dog's mouth, lips and tongue, while the dog may also experience vomiting, difficulty swallowing and drooling.

The plants noted above are only a few of the more common household plants, and every conscientious Dog guardian will want to educate themselves before bringing plants into the home that could be toxic to their canine companions.

3. Poison Proof Your Home

You can learn about many potentially toxic and poisonous sources both inside and outside your home by visiting the ASPCA Animal Poison Control Center website. Always keep your veterinarian's emergency number in a place where you can quickly access it, as well as the Emergency Poison Control telephone number, in case you suspect that your dog may have been poisoned.
Knowing what to do if you suspect your dog may have been poisoned and being able to quickly contact the right people could save your dog's life.
If you keep toxic cleaning substances (including fertilizers, vermin or snail poisons and vehicle products) in your home, garage or garden shed, always keep them behind closed doors. As well, keep any medications where your Miniature Golden Retriever can never get to them, and seriously consider eliminating the use of any and all toxic products, for the health of both yourself, your family and your best fur friends.

4. Garden Plants

Please note that there are also many outdoor plants that can be toxic or poisonous to your puppy or dog, therefore, always check what plants are growing in your garden and if any may be harmful, remove them or make certain that your Miniature Golden Retriever puppy or adult dog cannot eat them. Cornell University, Department of Animal Science lists many different categories of poisonous plants affecting dogs, including house plants, flower garden plants, vegetable garden plants, plants found in swamps or moist areas, plants found in fields, trees and shrubs, plants found in wooded areas, and ornamental plants.

5. Why Does My Dog Eat Grass?

Be aware that many puppies and adult dogs will eat grass, just because. Perhaps they like the taste, are curious, bored, or need a little moisture or fiber in their diet. Remember that canines are natural scavengers, always on the look out for something they can eat, and so long as the grass is healthy and has not been sprayed with toxic chemicals, a little grass eating should not be a concern.

6. Animal Poison Control Centers

The ASPCA Animal Poison Control Center is staffed 24 hours a day, 365 days a year and is a valuable resource for learning about what plants are toxic and possibly poisonous to your dog.

ASPCA Poison Control: www.aspca.org

a) USA Poison Emergency: Call: 1 (888) 426-4435
When calling the Poison Emergency number, your credit card may be charged with a $65 (£39.42) consultation fee.

b) UK Poison Emergency: Call: 0800-213-6680 - Pet Poison Helpline (payable service)

RSPCA: Call: 0300 1234 999

Chapter 16: Caring for Aging Dogs

1. What to Be Aware Of

As a result of many modern advances in veterinarian care, improvements in diet and nutrition and general knowledge concerning proper care of our canine companions, our dogs are able to enjoy longer, healthier lives.

As such, when caring for our canine companions, we need to be aware of behavioral and physical changes that will affect our dogs as they approach old age. While each dog's individual health, genetics, and spirit will affect how old they seem, and they may remain quite active as they get older, a Miniature Golden Retriever will be entering their senior years at around 10 to 12 years of age.

a) Physiological Changes: as our beloved canine companions enter into their senior years, they may be suffering from very similar physical aging problems that affect us humans, such as pain, stiffness and arthritis, and inability to control their bowels and bladder.

Any of these problems will reduce a dog's willingness to want to exercise.

b) Behavioral Changes: a senior Miniature Golden Retriever may experience behavioral changes resulting from loss of hearing and sight, such as disorientation, fear or startle reactions and overall grumpiness from any number of physical problems that could be causing them pain whenever they move.

Just as research and science has improved our human quality of life in our senior years, the same is becoming true for our canine counterparts who are able to benefit from dietary supplements and pharmaceutical products to help them be as comfortable as possible in their senior years.

Of course, there will be some inconveniences associated with keeping a dog with advancing years around the home, however, your Miniature Golden Retriever deserves no less than to spend their final days in your loving care after they have unconditionally given you their entire lives.

c) Geriatric Dogs: being aware of the changes that are occurring in a senior dog will help you to better care for them during their geriatric years.

For instance, most dogs will experience hearing loss and visual impairment, and how you help them will depend upon which goes first (hearing or sight).

If a dog's hearing is compromised, then using more hand signals will be helpful.

Deaf dogs will still be able to hear louder noises and feel vibrations, therefore hand clapping, knocking on walls, doors or furniture, using a loud clicker or stomping your foot on the floor may be a way to get their attention.

If a senior dog loses their eyesight, most dogs will still be able to easily navigate their familiar surroundings, and you will only need to be extra watchful on their behalf when taking them to unfamiliar territory.

If they still have their hearing, you will be able to assist your dog with verbal cues and commands. Dogs that have lost both their hearing and their sight will need to be close to you so that they can relax and not feel nervous, and so that you can communicate by touching parts of their body.

Generally speaking, even when a dog becomes blind and/or deaf, their powerful sense of smell is still functioning, which means that they will be able to smell where you are and navigate their environment by using their nose.

d) More Bathroom Breaks: bathroom breaks may need to become more frequent in older dogs who may lose their ability to hold it for longer periods of time, so be prepared to be more watchful and to offer them opportunities to go outside more frequently during the day.

You may also want to place a pee pad near the door, in case they just can't hold it long enough, or if you have not already taught them to go to the bathroom on an indoor potty patch, or pee pad, now may be the time for this alternative bathroom arrangement.

A dog who has been house trained for years will feel the shame and upset of not being able to hold it long enough to get to their regular bathroom location, so be kind and do whatever you need to do in order to help them not to have to feel bad about failing bowel or bladder control.

Our beloved canine companions may also begin to show signs of cognitive decline and changes in the way their brain functions, similar to what happens to humans suffering from Alzheimer's, where they start to wander about aimlessly, sometimes during the middle of the night. If your senior dog is wandering at night, make sure that they cannot accidentally fall down stairs or harm themselves in any way.

Being aware that an aging Miniature Golden Retriever will be experiencing many symptoms that are similar to an aging human will help you to understand how best to keep them safe and as comfortable as possible during this golden time in their lives.

2. How to Make Them Comfortable

a) Regular Checkups: during this time in your dog's life, when their immune systems become weakened and they may be experiencing pain, you will want to get into the habit of taking your senior Miniature Golden Retriever for regular veterinarian checkups.

Take them for a checkup every six months so that early detection of any problems can quickly be attended to and solutions for helping to keep your aging Miniature Golden Retriever comfortable can be provided.

b) No Rough Play: an older Miniature Golden Retriever will not have the same energy or willingness to play that they did when they were younger, therefore, do not allow younger children to rough house with an older dog. Explain to them that the dog is getting older and that as a result they must learn to be gentle and to leave the dog alone when it may want to rest or sleep.

c) Mild Exercise: dogs still love going for walks, even when they are getting older and slowing down. Although an older dog will generally have less energy, they still need to exercise and keep moving, and taking them out regularly for shorter or slower walks will keep them healthier and happier long into old age.

d) Best Quality Food: everyone has heard the saying, *"you are what you eat"* and for a senior dog, what he or she eats is even more important as his or her digestive system may no longer be functioning at peak performance.

Therefore, feeding a high quality, protein-based food will be important for a senior dog's continued health. As well, if your older Miniature Golden Retriever is overweight, you will want to help them shed excess pounds so that they will not be placing undue stress on their joints or heart.

The best way to accomplish this is by feeding smaller quantities of a higher quality food.

e) Clean and Parasite Free: the last thing an aging Miniature Golden Retriever should have to deal with is the misery of itching and scratching, so make sure that you continue to carefully give them regular baths with the appropriate shampoos and conditioners to keep their coat and skin comfortable and free from biting bugs.

f) Plenty of Water: proper hydration is essential for helping to keep an older dog comfortable. Water is life giving for every creature, so make certain that your aging dog has easy access to plenty of clean, fresh water which will help to improve their energy and digestion and also prevent dehydration which can add to joint stiffness.

g) Keep Them Warm: just as older humans feel the cold more, so do older dogs. Keeping your senior Miniature Golden Retriever warm will help to alleviate some of the pain of their joint stiffness or arthritis.

Make sure their bed or kennel is not kept in a drafty location and perhaps consider a heated bed for them. Be aware that your aging dog will be more sensitive to extremes in temperature, and it will be up to you to make sure that they are comfortable at all times, which means not too hot and not too cold.

h) Steps or Stairs: if your Miniature Golden Retriever is allowed to sleep on the human couch or chair, but they are having difficulties getting up there as their joints are becoming stiff and painful, consider buying or making them a set of soft, foam stairs so that they do not have to make the jump to their favorite sleeping place.

i) Comfortable Bed: while most dogs seem to be happy with sleeping on the floor, providing a padded, soft bed will greatly help to relieve sore spots and joint pain in older dogs. If there is a draft in the home, generally it will be at floor level, therefore, a bed that is raised up off of the floor will be warmer for your senior dog.

j) More Love and Attention: last, but not least, make sure that you give your senior dog lots of love and attention and never leave them alone for long periods of time. When they are not feeling their best, they will want to be with you all that much more because you are their trusted guardian whom they love beyond life itself.

3. What is Euthanasia?

Every veterinarian will have received special training to help provide all incurably ill, injured or aged pets that have come to the end of their natural lives with a humane and gentle death, through a process called *"euthanasia"*. When the time comes, euthanasia, or putting a dog *"to sleep"*, will usually be a two-step process.

First, the veterinarian will inject the dog with a sedative to make them sleepy, calm and comfortable.
Second, the veterinarian will inject a special drug that will peacefully stop their heart.

These drugs work in such a way that the dog will not experience any awareness whatsoever that his or her life is transitioning toward a peaceful ending.

What they will experience is very much like what we humans experience when falling asleep under anesthesia during a surgical procedure.

Once the second stage drug has been injected, the entire process takes about 10 to 20 seconds, at which time the veterinarian will then check to make certain that the dog's heart has stopped.

There is no suffering with this process, which is a very gentle and humane way to end a dog's suffering and allow them to peacefully pass on.

4. When to Help a Dog Transition

The impending loss of a beloved dog is one of the most painfully difficult and emotionally devastating experiences a canine guardian will ever have to face.

For the sake of our faithful companions, because we do not want to prolong their suffering, we humans will have to do our best to look at our dog's situation practically, rather than emotionally, so that we can make the best decision for them.

They may be suffering from extreme old age and the inability to even walk outside to relieve themselves, and thus having to deal with the indignity of regularly soiling their sleeping area, they may have been diagnosed with an incurable illness that is causing them much pain, or they may have been seriously injured.

Whatever the reason for a canine companion's suffering, it will be up to their human guardian to calmly guide the end-of-life experience so that any further discomfort and distress can be minimized.

5. What to Do If You Are Uncertain

In circumstances where it is not entirely clear how much a dog is suffering, it will be helpful to pay close attention to your dog's behavior and keep a daily log or record so that you can know for certain how much of their day is difficult and painful for them, and how much is not.

When you keep a daily log, it will be easier to decide if the dog's quality of life has become so poor that it makes better sense to offer them the gift of peacefully going to sleep.

During this time of uncertainty, it will also be very important to discuss with your veterinarian what signs of suffering may be associated with the dog's particular disease or condition, so that you know what to look for.

Often a dog may still continue to eat or drink despite being upset, having difficulty breathing, excessively panting, being disoriented or in much pain, and as their caring guardians, we will have to weigh their love of eating against how much they are really suffering in all other aspects of their life.

Obviously, if a canine guardian can clearly see that their beloved companion is suffering throughout their days and nights, it will make sense to help humanely end their suffering by planning a euthanasia procedure.

We humans are often tempted to delay the inevitable moment of euthanasia, because we love our dogs so much and cannot bear the anticipation of the intense grief we know will overwhelm us when we must say our final goodbyes to our beloved fur friend.

Unfortunately, we may regret that we allowed our dog to suffer too long, and could find ourselves wishing that if only we humans had the same option, to peacefully let go, when in our own lives, we find ourselves in such a position.

6. Grieving a Lost Friend

Some humans do not fully recognize the terrible grief involved in losing a beloved canine friend. There will be many who do not understand the close bond we humans can have with our dogs, which is often unlike any we have with our human counterparts.

Your friends may give you pitying looks and try to cheer you up, but if they have never experienced such a loss themselves, they may also secretly think that you are making too much fuss over "just a dog".

For some of us humans, the loss of a beloved dog is so painful that we decide never to share our lives with another, because we cannot bear the thought of going through the pain of loss again.

Expect to feel terribly sad, tearful and yes, depressed because those who are close to their canine companions will feel their loss no less acutely than the loss of a human friend or life partner. The grieving process can take some time to recover from, and some of us never totally recover.

After the loss of a family dog, first you need to take care of yourself by making certain that you keep eating and getting regular sleep, even though you will feel an almost eerie sense of loneliness.

Losing a beloved dog is a serious shock to the system, which can also affect your concentration and your ability to find joy or want to participate in other activities that may be part of your daily life.

During this early grieving time you will need to take extra care while driving or performing tasks that require your concentration as you may find yourself distracted.

If there are other dogs or pets in the home, they will also be grieving the loss of a companion, and may display this by acting depressed, being off their food or showing little interest in play or games. Therefore, you need to help guide your other pets through this grieving process by keeping them busy and interested, taking them for extra walks and spending more time with them.

Many people do not wait long enough before attempting to replace a lost pet and will immediately go to the local shelter and rescue a deserving dog. While this may help to distract you from your grieving process, this is not really fair to the new fur member of your family.

Bringing a new pet into a home that is depressed and grieving the loss of a long time canine member may create behavioral problems for the new dog who will be faced with learning all about their new home while also dealing with the unstable, sad energy of the grieving family.

A better scenario would be to allow yourself the time to properly grieve by waiting a minimum of one month to allow yourself and your family to feel happier and more stable before deciding upon sharing your home with another dog.

The grieving process will be different for everyone and you will know when the time is right to consider sharing your home with another canine companion.

7. The Rainbow Bridge Poem

"Just this side of heaven is a place called Rainbow Bridge.
When an animal dies that has been especially close to someone here,
that pet goes to Rainbow Bridge.
There are meadows and hills for all of our special friends
so they can run and play together.
There is plenty of food, water and sunshine,
and our friends are warm and comfortable.

All animals who had been ill and old are restored to health and vigor;
those who were hurt or maimed are made whole and strong again,
just as we remember them in our dreams of days and times gone by.
The animals are happy and content, except for one small thing;
they each miss someone very special to them, who had to be left behind.

They all run and play together,
but the day comes when one suddenly stops
and looks into the distance.
His bright eyes are intent; His eager body quivers.
Suddenly he begins to run from the group,
flying over the green grass, his legs carrying him faster and faster.

You have been spotted,
and when you and your special friend finally meet,
you cling together in joyous reunion, never to be parted again.
The happy kisses rain upon your face; your hands again caress the beloved

head, and you look once more into the trusting eyes
of your pet, so long gone from your life
but never absent from your heart.

Then you cross Rainbow Bridge together...."

- Author unknown

8. Memorials

There are as many ways to honor the passing of a beloved pet, as each of our furry friends is uniquely special to us.

For instance, you and your family may wish to have your companion cremated and preserve their ashes in a special urn or sprinkle their ashes along their favorite walk, or across the lake where they loved to swim.

Perhaps you will want to have a special marker, photo bereavement, photo engraved Rainbow Bridge Poem, or wooden plaque created in honor of your passed friend, or you may wish to keep their memory close to you at all times by having a DNA remembrance pendant or bracelet designed.

As well, there are support groups, such as Rainbow Bridge, which is a grief support community, to help you and your family through this painful period of loss and grief.

Chapter 17: Rescue Organizations

When you are considering rescuing a specific breed of dog or puppy, the first place to start your search will be with your local breeders, shelters and rescue groups.

There are many breed specific rescue organizations in Canada, the USA, the United Kingdom and many other countries and the easiest way to find one closest to you is to go online and type in the breed name of the dog you want to rescue next to the name of the city where you live.

1. Shelters

Here you can expect to pay an adoption fee to cover the cost of spaying or neutering, but this will be only a small percentage of what you would pay a breeder, and you will be saving a life at the same time.

2. Online Resources

Sites such as Petango, Adopt A Pet and Pet Finder can be good places to begin your search. Each of these online resources is a central gathering site for hundreds and hundreds of local shelters, humane societies and rescue groups.

3. Canine Clubs and Breeders

Another place to search will be clubs or breeders in your local area. These groups may have rescue dogs available.

Chapter 18: Resources & References

The following resources and references are listed alphabetically within their specific category and include web addresses.

1. Poison Control

ASPCA Poison Control: www.aspca.org

Poisonous Plants Affecting Dogs - Cornell University, Department of Animal Science: www.ansi.cornell.edu/plants/dogs/

2. Breeders, Registries & Rescues

Adopt A Pet: www.adoptapet.com
Comfort Retrievers: www.comfortretrievers.com
Designer Dogs – The Kennel Club: www.thekennelclub.org.uk
Miniature Golden Retriever: www.miniaturegoldenretriever.net
National Dog Tattoo Register: www.dog-register.co.uk
National Dog Registry: www.nationaldogregistry.com
Petango: www.petango.com
Pet Finder: www.petfinder.com
The American Canine Hybrid Club: www.achclub.com
The International Designer Canine Registry: www.designercanineregistry.com
The National Hybrid Registry: www.nationalhybridregistry.com

3. Equipment, Supplies & Services

Andis Dog Clippers: www.andis.com
Dog Bowl for Your Dog: www.dogbowlforyourdog.com
Dremel™ Nail Grinder for Dogs: www.dremel.com
K-9 Super Heroes Dog Whispering: www.k-9superheroesdogwhispering.com
Mim VarioCage: www.mightymitedoggear.com
Must Have Publishing: www.musthavepublishing.com
Modern Puppies: www.modernpuppies.com
Oster Dog Clippers: www.osterpro.com
Potty Patch: www.pottypatch.com
Poochie Bells™: www.poochie-pets.net

Remove Urine Odors: www.removeurineodors.com
Sleepy Pod: www.sleepypod.com
Springer Bicycle Jogger: available online
Tell Bell™: www.tellbell.com
Tick Twister: www.ticktwister.com
ThunderShirt: www.thundershirt.com
Wahl Dog Clippers: www.wahl.com

4. Memorials

Rainbow Bridge: www.rainbowbridge.com

Published by PESA Publishing 2017

Printed in Great Britain
by Amazon

55778657R00104